True Tales *of the* Olympic Peninsula

True Tales of the Olympic Peninsula

Carol Turner

Published by The History Press
Charleston, SC
www.historypress.com

Cover image: Olympic Mountains. *Photo by Bill Baccus, courtesy of the National Park Service.*

First published 2024

Manufactured in the United States

ISBN 9781467154628

Library of Congress Control Number: 2023950643

For Naama and the others.

CONTENTS

ACKNOWLEDGEMENTS

I owe many thanks to the wonderful folks at the North Olympic Library System (NOLS) in Port Angeles. This book is filled with images, stories and tidbits from its collection of books, archived documents and photographs. Thanks in particular to NOLS for its generosity in allowing me to use images from the Bert Kellogg Photograph Collection, found on the North Olympic Heritage website. I could not have created this book without having that access. And kudos to the late Bert Kellogg himself for building that amazing collection. It is truly a wealth of history that has been scanned and posted online for all to see.

I also received help from the folks at North Olympic History Center, particularly in my hunt for the history of Mora. I am also grateful for assistance from folks who provided images from other collections: Caitlin Alcorn and Molly Woolbright at University of Washington Press, Ruba Sadi at University of Washington Libraries Special Collections and Reed Barry at Jefferson County Historical Society. I am also grateful to the Library of Congress, Prints & Photographs Division, and the National Park Service for the use of their images. Alison Costanza at the Washington State Archives Northwest Region helped dig up and copy for me the case file for the lawsuit against the men from Dungeness.

Thanks also to my friend Sarah Miller, keeper of the Henry Blake flame and longtime volunteer and caretaker at the New Dungeness Lighthouse. Sarah shared photographs from the New Dungeness Lighthouse collection as well as her insight into the history of the lighthouse and its first keeper, Henry Blake.

Special mention is due to the late Makah artist Lance Wilkie for installing the memorial at the Ozette archaeological site.

Others who helped along the way include Darryl Beckmann; Phil Gruen; Melissa Calloway; Brian Atwater at University of Washington; Bryon Monohon, director of the Forks Timber Museum; and Valerie Soe.

Finally, I'd like to thank Laurie Krill at The History Press, who has been a pleasure to work with, and my fun companion on research trips, Elizabeth Clarke.

Chapter 1

THE COCKEYED SAGA OF *THE EGG AND I*

1927 and 1945

The year was 1945 and the world was sick of war. People in the Allied nations rejoiced at their hard-won victory over the Axis powers of World War II. In New York City, a major publisher, J. Lippincott Inc., was finalizing touches on a humorous memoir written by a first-time author named Betty MacDonald. The popular magazine *Atlantic Monthly* had already serialized the book, publishing one chapter per month. The book was called *The Egg and I*, and its publication would change the life of its thirty-eight-year-old author.

In *The Egg and I*, Betty tells her story, beginning with her upbringing as part of a fun, raucous and intellectual family. In the late 1920s, Betty meets a handsome stranger, Bob, and the two of them get married and move to a remote chicken farm near today's Chimacum. In easy-to-read prose that is whimsical, funny and self-deprecating, Betty describes her battles against the rain, cold and mold, not to mention the chirping hordes of hungry chicks that overwhelmed her daily life. On top of all that, she had a baby girl to care for. Her closest friend and enemy was "Stove," the ancient and temperamental kitchen monster that refused to keep her and her tiny daughter warm and stubbornly prevented her from making edible bread. Her distracted husband, Bob, was forever slaving away outside—building barns and chicken coops, fixing fences, battling cougars and bears and making big plans that would inevitably create a lot more work for her.

The book was an immediate and massive success. Lippincott cranked out so many printings to keep up with demand that the continuing postwar shortage of paper and cloth for binding meant it had to put aside other books in its catalogue. Reviewers declared that that Betty's war-weary readers related to the difficulties and unremitting battles of her life on the farm—a desperate struggle to survive that was all too familiar to many during the war years. More importantly, Betty served up to her readers a great feast of comic relief. She had a profound talent for biting humor that inspired "scream[ing] with helpless mirth," as described by a former co-worker who had listened to Betty tell the stories before the book's publication. Betty's sense of humor was clever, imperious and stinging. Scattered among the many scenes of slapstick comedy were visits with her zany, thick-headed and homely neighbors, the Kettles and the Hickses. Although she made fun of herself and her numerous domestic failings as a twenty-year-old kid completely out of her depth, she reserved her most cutting commentary for those neighbors.

On December 23, 1945, *The Egg and I* reached number one on the *New York Times* nonfiction bestseller list. It remained there for forty-three weeks. After that, it settled in the top five for seven more months. *LIFE* magazine published a full-blown feature on Betty and her family, who had long since left the Olympic Peninsula. Betty was now in her late thirties. She and her new husband, Don MacDonald, toured the country for book events and were fêted by the rich and powerful. On August 15, 1946, the millionth copy of her book was ceremoniously handed over to Betty, who quipped, "Thanks a million!" It was one of the most successful first books of all time, and soon there was a movie deal.

Famed actress Claudette Colbert, at the peak of her stardom at the time, won the lead role as Betty. Bob would be played by another favorite actor, Fred MacMurray. As it turned out, even more important (and eventually more lucrative for Hollywood) was the casting of Ma and Pa Kettle—Marjorie Main and Percy Kilbride. The movie was a huge hit and spawned nine additional films, although the focus of the stories changed. In the subsequent films, the wacky antics of Ma and Pa Kettle and their families took over, while Betty and Bob disappeared from the stories. The films reportedly grossed Universal Studios $35 million (almost half a billion in today's dollars) and saved the studio from an impending bankruptcy.

Meanwhile, Betty and Don MacDonald enjoyed their financial windfall. They traveled, went to parties and mingled with movie stars. Betty continued writing and produced two more humorous memoirs about her life, plus a children's series called *Mrs. Piggly Wiggly*. Their exciting and happy lives were a far cry from the misery, instability and brutality that had actually characterized Betty's life on the Chimacum farm with her first husband, Bob Heskett.

Betty MacDonald, née Elizabeth Bard, was born in Boulder, Colorado, in 1907. Her father, Darsie Bard, was a mining engineer whose work frequently took him away from the family for prolonged periods. When Betty was nine, her father finally settled down into a teaching position in Seattle. The family of six—three daughters and one son—prospered there. Darsie Bard made a good living and soon became a prominent member of Seattle society. They lived in a fine house in Seattle's Laurelhurst neighborhood. The two older girls, Betty and Mary, went to a private prep school, with plans to earn college degrees from the University of Washington.

Tragedy struck in January 1920 when Darsie Bard died suddenly of pneumonia. His wife, Sydney, was pregnant at the time. After Darsie's death, the family's daily life became an ongoing financial struggle. Sydney was plagued by unscrupulous operators who cheated her out of income generated by property that Darsie had left her. The girls had to leave the private school and switch to Lincoln High School. Their plans for a college education were cut off, and they each managed only a year or two at the University of Washington.

Despite the ongoing hardships, the Bard family was a lively and happy one. Sydney took her difficulties in stride. According to family friends, the atmosphere in the Bard household was full of fun, intellect, teasing and sometimes preposterous plans and schemes. Sydney opened a tearoom called the Mandarin, where the older kids worked. Unfortunately, the place went out of business.

In 1926, the family decided to become farmers, and they bought a property on the Olympic Peninsula in an area known as Center, near Chimacum. None of them knew anything about farming. The move to such a remote, rural setting was a shocker after the modern, open society of Jazz Age Seattle. They muddled along, doing their best to raise chickens, with the son, Cleve Bard, supposedly in charge of the slapdash operation. Reportedly, many of Betty's later stories about life on the farm came from this happier period when she lived with her own family—before Bob Heskett.

Betty was only seventeen when her brother brought home the tall, handsome Bob Heskett. Mary Bard, Betty's elder sister, said he looked like the movie star Gary Cooper. Bob was a thirty-year-old World War I Marine Corps veteran and worked as an insurance agent. In 1927, the smitten Betty became a "child bride," as her maternal grandmother dubbed her.

Betty's family wasn't present at the ceremony, so the two may have eloped. Seven months later, in February 1928, their daughter Anne Heskett was born. (It's possible, if not likely, that the timing pointed at an urgency to marry.)

In January 1928, the Bard family farm in Chimacum was foreclosed on due to a series of bad actors involved in a complicated mortgage scheme that Sydney had signed up for. However, a few months later, Sydney settled a lawsuit around another property that her husband had left her, which resulted in payments to each of the Bard children. This sudden windfall allowed newlyweds Bob and Betty Heskett to buy their own Chimacum farm. Sydney and the rest of the family (except the eldest, Mary) found a place to rent in Jefferson County, not far from Bob, Betty and baby Anne. In July 1929, Betty gave birth again, to their second daughter, Joan Dorothy Heskett, in Port Townsend.

Bob Heskett didn't know anything about farming either, and he turned out to be a very bad husband indeed. Their life on the farm and their relationship bore no resemblance to the life and marriage depicted in the alleged "nonfiction" memoir *The Egg and I*. It's not clear how much Betty's family knew about what was really going on. Decades later, one of the Hesketts' neighbors, Bud Bishop, sat for an oral history interview with a volunteer at the Jefferson County Historical Society, who asked him about his famous former neighbor. "'Betty was usually left alone with her two little girls,' Bud remembered. 'I cut her wood and got bark and stuff off the stumps for her in the winter time because her husband was a bum. He was either drunk or making moonshine, and she was up there with two little baby girls, and she couldn't get wood so I went up there and got wood for her to keep them from freezing.'"[1]

Betty's young sister Dede often visited the farm to help out, and she witnessed Bob's behavior but was too young to do anything about it. In her humorous narrative in *The Egg and I*, Betty provides the occasional offhand hint about her real life with the "bum":

> "[W]*ho, me?" I asked, when we were moving and Bob pointed casually to a large chest of drawers and said, "Carry that into the bedroom."*
>
> *"Who else?" he snapped and my lower lip began to tremble because I knew now that I was just a wife.*[2]

She described herself as "alternat[ing] between delirious happiness and black despair."

Above: Farm, Chimacum, from *The Egg and I.* The farmhouse was torn down in 1958. *Collection of the Jefferson County Historical Society, #2005.69.19.*

Right: Woman, probably Betty Bard Heskett, with baby, probably Anne Heskett, summer of 1928. *University of Washington Libraries, Special Collections, SOC13937.*

In another scene from *The Egg and I*, Betty is outside working in the field with Bob when a horse steps on her foot: "'She's on my foot,' I said mildly to Bob who was complaining because we had stopped. 'Get her off and let's get going,' shouted the man who had promised to cherish me. Meanwhile my foot was being driven like a stake into the soft earth."[3] But for the most part, the Bob in *The Egg and I* is hardworking, always busy and doing admirable work.

Betty's biographer was candid about Bob's bad behavior and suggested that it may have been related to postwar PTSD: "By this time the romance of her marriage to Bob had dissipated. Betty never knew when or why she ceased to charm Bob, or what about her might have irked him. That Bob had been a soldier and endured the horrors of the battlefield may have played into his impatience, but she could do nothing about that except stay out of his way."[4]

Bob did have one passion during those years, and that was distilling moonshine and drinking his product. He appeared to have several partners in this business, including one or more local Native Americans. *The Egg and I* includes a good number of jarringly racist comments on Betty's part about Native Americans, whom she dismissed using negative stereotypes and terms such as "squaw." She has them staying in "wigwams, or wherever they lived." Today, her stark bigotry would have prevented the publication of *The Egg and I*, but it was acceptable to the white reading public of the 1940s and '50s, as well as to Betty herself, who declared in plain terms, "I do not like Indians!" In one of her few specific complaints, she recounts being menaced by one of her husband's Native American drinking buddies, who showed up drunk in her kitchen when she was alone in the house with her kids.

In the fall of 1930, a year after the stock market crash that brought on the Great Depression, the Bard family left their Chimacum farm and moved back to Seattle. Also that summer, Betty left her husband, moved in with her sister Mary in Seattle with her two little girls and initiated divorce proceedings in King County against Bob. She was twenty-three.

It took her five years to finalize this divorce, during which she gave Bob several more chances to straighten up after he pleaded with her. When they finally split up, divorce documents show that the farm and the seven hundred chickens belonged to Betty since they were purchased with her inheritance. The papers also provide insight to the real nature of that relationship:

> *Although Bob was able bodied, Betty alleged, he had done nothing to support his family other than taking on a small amount of work on the farm.*

> *At all times since said marriage the defendant has treated the plaintiff in a cruel and inhuman manner and subjected her to such personal indignities as to render life burdensome; that the defendant has on numerous occasions violently beaten plaintiff and used toward her other personal violence; And defendant has on many occasions used toward plaintiff violent and abusive language, and subjected her to insults in the presence of members of her family and friends. That during all of said time defendant has been and now is an habitual drunkard.*[5]

A second set of divorce documents created after a temporary change of heart describe Bob's behavior in even worse terms:

> *Said defendant has struck and kicked plaintiff on a number of occasions and has threatened to shoot plaintiff and the children. At one time said defendant poured coal oil on the side of the house and set it afire and it was only by timely discovery by plaintiff and her younger sister that destruction of the house and injury to the family was prevented. Without justification or cause by plaintiff, said defendant has repeatedly called plaintiff vile names and has threatened to disfigure plaintiff so that no one else would ever care for her. Said defendant has become addicted to the use of intoxicating liquors and frequently during the said marriage has become drunken and abusive toward plaintiff and just before plaintiff's first child was born defendant struck and kicked her. And during all of the said married life said defendant has been brutal with, and abusive of, plaintiff.*[6]

After finally leaving Bob for good, Betty found employment beginning in 1933 with the National Recovery Administration, part of President Franklin Delano Roosevelt's "New Deal," which supplied the operations of the Works Progress Administration (WPA). However, more bad luck came her way in 1938 when she contracted pulmonary tuberculosis at the age of thirty-one and had to enter the Firland Sanitorium just north of Seattle. Her daughters stayed with her mother, Sydney Bard, while Betty fought to recover. The family's financial struggles worsened with this setback, as they had become dependent on Betty's income.

While at the sanitorium, she had to go through a painful procedure called artificial pneumothorax to prevent her lung from collapsing. In a later memoir, she described it as "suffocating." She was in bed for seven months and was finally discharged another two months later. During her illness, she had started to write, keeping a detailed journal of her experiences. She tried to publish a manuscript but had no luck.

A few years later, her fortunes improved when she met Don MacDonald, whom she married in April 1942. Don worked at Boeing. At the time, it was illegal in Washington State for anyone under forty-five diagnosed with tuberculosis to marry, so they went up to Everett, where nobody knew them.

The new family moved to Vashon Island in the fall of 1942. Betty had for years entertained family and friends with hilarious stories, many of them based on her life back in Chimacum. Her sister Mary prodded her to turn the stories into a manuscript, a project that Betty had started but put aside in favor of her new marriage. Still, Mary had a friend at Doubleday Duran & Company, a major publisher, who was shopping for new authors. Betty called in sick to work on an outline, and Mary's publishing friend showed interest. Unfortunately, or perhaps fortunately, Betty got caught for calling in sick and was fired, so she devoted her unemployed days to the manuscript. She did not hear from the editor for many months, and she took another job, putting the manuscript on the back burner again. A few years passed before she finally finished writing. The original editor had moved on by then, but Betty sent it to a prominent literary agent, Bernice Baumgarten at Brandt and Brandt in New York City. Baumgarten agreed to represent her and helped her rework the material from the diary format into a narrative.

Betty's original manuscript was reportedly more candid about the bad relationship with Bob, but Baumgarten insisted that she needed to clean it up. In developing the "Bob" in the book, Betty began using the character of her current husband, Don, as a much more palatable and lovable model. It wasn't long before the real "Bob" was almost entirely eliminated from the story in all but name. Nevertheless, the publisher marketed the book as a nonfiction memoir.

When the film came along, the icy cleanliness of Claudette Colbert and wholesomeness of Fred MacMurray further chipped away at the toxic reality of Betty's former life at the Heskett farm in Chimacum. The final product was sweet and silly, and even the yokel neighbors and drunken Native Americans received a cleansing.

Meanwhile, the film producers had the actual, living Bob Heskett to contend with. By then, many years had passed, and he owed Betty $5,500 in back child support payments. The film company approached him and offered to pay off that debt, along with a bonus of $1,000. Heskett signed away all rights to his name and story, probably grateful that his egregious behavior had been through such a thorough laundering.

Betty MacDonald (*left*) and Claudette Colbert, in Hollywood, for the film version of *The Egg and I*, 1946. *University of Washington Libraries, Special Collections, SOC13893.*

The studio executives did not bother to get similar waivers from Betty's former neighbors, but they had done such a good job in removing Betty's written venom in the translation from book to film that they had little to worry about.

In the film, Betty becomes friends with Ma Kettle, and everyone demonstrates a good-humored tolerance of Pa Kettle's habit of "borrowing" items. Betty goes to great lengths to help their eldest son get money for college. She is a loving, friendly neighbor. Much of the film's plot revolves around a predatory vixen trying to steal Bob away from Betty—a character who did not exist in the book.

The book was a different story. Her treatment of her neighbors, not to mention the Native Americans, was far more acerbic than the film's approach. In the book, Pa Kettle was a "lazy, lisping sonofabitch." Ma Kettle was presented as a grotesque figure with an enormous shifting bosom and a pottymouth. Her home was an asylum of screaming kids, chickens and squalor, and she gives a long, matter-of-fact speech about how all of her fifteen kids "had fits" (seizures).

Publicity photograph of the Kettle family, for the film version of *The Egg and I*, 1946. *University of Washington Libraries, Special Collections, SOC13904.*

Another family, the Hickses, were also cartoonish: "Mr. Hicks, a large ruddy dullard, walked gingerly through life, being very careful not to get dirt on anything or in any way to irritate Mrs. Hicks, whom he regarded as a cross between Mary Magdalene and the County Agent."[7] Mrs. Hicks was also a hypochondriac who spoke about little else besides "her liver and her bile."

Betty had told interviewers that the characters were composites of numerous people she had known or heard about, that they weren't based on specific people. She mentioned to a radio personality that she had never been back to Chimacum after writing the book and that her neighbors wouldn't care about any of it. If she assumed that nobody in Chimacum would read it, she was mistaken. All the publicity around the book and film turned the area into a tourist destination. Carloads of visitors arrived in Jefferson County hoping to see the Heskett farm, and someone put up a sign near the ferry dock pointing the way.

The spread was now owned by Anita and Alfred Larson, who were relatives by marriage of the neighboring Bishop family. The house that

Betty and Bob had lived in was being used as a chicken house. Locals pointed the way to the Larson home, and Anita Larson charged one dollar to let people come and gawk at things that were in the book, including the "Stove" that had such an outsized role in the young Betty's life. Anita Larson kept a guest book that eventually contained signatures from residents of more than sixty countries.

If Betty had originally downplayed the danger of upsetting neighbors who recognized themselves in the book, her publisher had foreseen the possibility of financial peril. Before the book was published, they had changed the original name of her neighbors from Basket (too close to Bishop) to Kettle. She used a pen name of B.B. MacDonald. They changed the name of Port Townsend to "Town," Port Ludlow became "Docktown" and the "Olympic Peninsula" became the "Pacific Coast" or simply "the mountains." Hood Canal became "Canal." These changes were all insisted on by the publisher. Perhaps Betty eventually began to sense a vulnerability because she tried to dissuade a film location scout from visiting the area, fearing that it would stir things up.

Despite these efforts, on March 25, 1947, Betty's former Chimacum neighbors, Edward and Ilah Bishop, filed a lawsuit against Betty and Don MacDonald, demanding $100,000. They claimed that they were the couple referred to as Mr. and Mrs. Hicks and that the book was libelous and an invasion of their privacy. They said they had been exposed to ridicule, hatred and contempt.

The Bishops had been the Hesketts' nearest neighbor, and it was their son Bud who had tried to help Betty when Bob was off drinking. The father, Edward, had been a logger and longshoreman but broke his back in an accident in 1930. They raised chickens, selling about thirty thousand per year. Their complaint pointed out every section of the book that mentioned the Hickses.

Outraged by the lawsuit, Betty vented her frustration in a letter to her agent:

> *I wanted to show how magnificent the country is in comparison with the unsavoryness of its inhabitants…*[N]*ow I wonder if perhaps my youth, inexperience, loneliness and upbringing didn't make me think the people were worse than they were—perhaps if I were able to move out there now I wouldn't be as discouraged, as lonely and as cold but would find the people less horrifying, more amusing. Perhaps the book would have a better flavor if I were to forget the truth and make the people less like the ignorant, immoral, unmoral, foul-mouthed group they were, and more folksy and*

> *quaint. If depicting the people as they were is libelous, then by all means let's show them as they weren't.*[8]

In May 1949, as Betty was working on her third book, she settled the case for $1,500. Edward and Ilah Bishop signed a release. Betty thought that her troubles were over, but three months later, the patriarch of the Bishop family, Albert Bishop, and ten others filed individual libel suits, claiming that they had been used as the Kettle family in *The Egg and I*. In addition to Albert, the plaintiffs included six of his sons, two daughters and one daughter-in-law. Furthermore, another Chimacum resident, an Indigenous man named Raymond Johnson, also filed suit, claiming that he was the Indian character Betty called "Crowbar."

All the lawsuits alleged that their depictions in the book subjected them to shame and humiliation. The defendants included Betty and her husband, Don; Lippincott; Pocketbooks, which had issued a twenty-five-cent paperback; and the Bon Marché department store, which sold the books. Each suit asked for damages of $100,000, except for Johnson, who asked for $75,000.

Betty admitted to her lawyer that 90 percent of what she wrote about "Paw Kettle" (changed in the film to "Pa Kettle") did come from information she'd heard about Albert Bishop, "whom she remembered as a principal topic of conversation on the Olympic peninsula. It was true she conceded that Albert Bishop had a lisp and the same vocal tic (his voice rose at the end of his sentences) with which she endowed Paw Kettle."[9]

This time, Betty refused to settle, and the trial in King County began on February 5, 1951. Albert Bishop was eighty-seven and was too ill to appear. Bon Marché Inc. was dismissed immediately as a defendant, and it turned out that Pocketbooks had never been served. Over the two-week trial, the judge constantly referred to a copy of the book on his desk. Most of the discussion centered on similarities between characters in the book and the plaintiffs. Betty's attorney pointed out how much money the locals had been making off the tourists and how the locals had initially enjoyed the attention and were proud of their newfound fame.

At the end of the trial, the judge instructed the jury that the suffering and humiliation of the plaintiffs only occurred in cases where people who read the book actually knew those neighbors. He declared that the vast majority of readers had no idea who any of these people were.

When the jury went out, they read the entire book, which took twenty-four hours. They then took a vote, and the result was unanimous in favor of the defendants. Betty had won.

Meanwhile, the same year of Betty's trial, on July 24, 1951, fifty-five-year-old Robert E. Heskett was stabbed to death in his apartment by Thomas J. Blake, thirty-seven, a bulldozer operator. Heskett had been working as a carpenter in Oakland, California. Blake's estranged (or perhaps ex-) wife had moved into Heskett's apartment a week earlier with her two daughters. Blake found out and arrived at the apartment, demanding to see his "babies." A fight ensued, and Blake stabbed Heskett to death.

In August 1956, Betty was diagnosed with endometriosis. During a related surgery, they discovered that she had ovarian cancer. After a two-year battle, Betty MacDonald died on February 7, 1958, at the age of fifty.

Chapter 2

THE PRIVATE WAR OF DANIEL PULLEN

1860s to 1890s

During the summer of 1887, folks in La Push, Washington, witnessed the rise of a grand oddity—a Victorian-style mansion perched near a blustery beach on the outer coast of the Olympic Peninsula. Situated in a remote region surrounded on three sides by a dense barrier of rainforest and mountains, the ostentatious house was the masterpiece of a driven white man from Maine named Daniel Pullen.

As he labored away on his mansion, Pullen found himself fenced in by more than just natural barriers. He was also under siege by the U.S. Department of Interior, by the local Indian agent stationed in Neah Bay, by members of the Quileute tribe and even by some of his white neighbors and family members.

Pullen had been upsetting people for a long time. Since he arrived in the area fifteen years before, he had—by hook or by crook—seized for himself every chunk of land he could. Some of the land was previously unclaimed; much of it was spoken for. In fact, he was building his mansion right in the middle of the Quileute village, and he had bullied aside his Quileute neighbors to do it. Pullen's attitude was so dismissive of the Quileute and anyone else who tried to get in his way that he eventually engineered his own downfall. By the time he finally got his comeuppance, he had unintentionally galvanized momentous changes in the La Push region, not the least of which was the federal government finally creating the Quileute Reservation. In the end, Pullen was left with nothing.

Above: The Pullen mansion at La Push, with family members in foreground, 1890s. Unknown photographer. *Bert Kellogg Collection of the North Olympic Library System.*

Right: Daniel Webster Pullen. *Photo by Peterson & Bro., Photography, Seattle, Washington, Bert Kellogg Collection of the North Olympic Library System.*

Daniel Webster Pullen was born in Maine in 1842. He survived a rough childhood during which his family was struck with scarlet fever when he was seven. His father and elder sister died. The fever deafened two of his other siblings and severely damaged his own hearing. Afterward, his mother somehow supported her family of eight surviving children.

At the start of the Civil War in April 1861, Daniel was nineteen years old. Congress did not impose conscription into the Northern army until 1863, and it's likely that he had already headed to the Pacific Northwest by then, following his brother Mart. At that time, the most common route from the East to West Coast was to take a passenger ship down to Panama, traverse the isthmus via railroad and catch another steamer up the West Coast to San Francisco and beyond.

Daniel Pullen first appears in regional records working at a Port Gamble logging camp as a bull puncher. A bull puncher drove a team of oxen, generally using a hickory stick and a steel goad (a spear-like instrument with a sharp hook) to "encourage" the oxen to pull or drag logs. During that period, Daniel earned a reputation for his severe methods of controlling the oxen.

Meanwhile, Dan's brother Mart had been living in Neah Bay on the Makah Reservation (established in 1855), working as a ship's pilot. In 1865, Daniel and Mart bought a pilot schooner, a small boat used to carry local pilots back and forth to visiting ships. Daniel began a new career as a skipper of the pilot schooner, transferring Mart back and forth to ships so he could steer them through the labyrinthine and treacherous waters of Puget Sound. Daniel also began using the schooner to set up a trade operation with the Quileutes, who provided him with seal skins and furs. In exchange, he brought the Quileutes desirable items such as cloth, sugar and tobacco. (The federal government banned the sale of alcohol to Native Americans in the 1820s.)

In the early 1870s, Daniel and Mart each filed land claims in an area known as the Quillayute Prairie or Fern Prairie. It was a flat, fertile plain about twelve miles northeast of La Push, located between the Dickey, Sol Duc and Quillayute Rivers (near today's Quillayute Airport). For centuries, the Quileutes had used the area to forage for camas and fern roots. The tribe kept the prairie clear of trees by annual burning, which also created prime grazing ground for deer and elk. In the eyes of a settler hoping to hunt, farm and ranch without having to first log the area and pull up massive root balls, it was plum territory. And the federal government had not protected it for the Quileutes.

Back in 1856, the Quileutes had signed a Chinook-language treaty with Governor Isaac Stevens. Chinook was a trade jargon originally used by regional tribes to communicate and later adopted by white traders. It consisted of about five hundred words, which did not allow for much clarity or delicacy. In the treaty, the Quileute tribe was assigned to the Quinault Reservation farther south. It's not clear whether Stevens and his aides knew or cared that the small Quileute tribe of fewer than three hundred was not part of the Quinault Nation:

> *Although European traders had previously made contact with Quileutes as early as the 1700s, the first official contacts were made in 1855 when the Quileutes signed a treaty* [Treaty of Quinault River] *with staff members of Washington Territory governor, Isaac Stevens. A year later, a Quileute delegation traveled to Olympia to sign a treaty* [Treaty of Olympia] *with the United States. According to that treaty, the Quileutes were to give up their lands and move to a reservation at Taholah. However, so remote was Quileute territory that there was little pressure to settle their lands.*[10]

The treaty not only failed to protect the Quileute homeland but also partnered the Quileutes with the Quinaults instead of their actual relatives, the Chimacums. It left the Quileutes without protection. Quileute leaders later claimed that they did not know they were expected to give up their lands:

> [T]*he paper that they signed was explained to them to be an agreement to keep the peace with citizens of the United States, and to accord them the same rights to come into their country and trade for furs, &c. as had previously been accorded to the Hudson Bay Company, and that the presents and payments in goods that they then received, and have since been receiving, were believed by them to be in consideration of their observance of that agreement.*[11]

This confusion, or disagreement, all too typical at the time of Euro-American expansion, lay at the root of any conflicts between the Quileutes and white settlers. However, in this case, clashes were rare. The feds did not sweep in and insist that the Quileutes move to the Quinault Reservation. The Quileutes went on with their lives on their usual and accustomed territory. They maintained a balance of trade and peaceful coexistence with a scattering of white settlers—except in the case of Daniel Pullen.

Pullen spent the 1870s continuing his trade activities and expanding his acquisition of land claims. He built a modest house and a barn on the Quillayute Prairie and raised cattle. His "bull-punching" personality brought him attention when a newspaper article described his method of keeping wolves away from his cattle—by killing a pig, infusing it with strychnine and leaving it out for the wolves to eat. (Wolves went extinct on the peninsula in the 1890s.)

The mid-1870s also saw the arrival in the area of a new family of settlers originally from Maine, one who would change Daniel Pullen's life and have a major impact on the village of La Push: Andrew Jackson Smith and his wife and children.

A.J. Smith came to Neah Bay in 1876 to take a job as Indian agent at the Makah Agency. Over the preceding decades, Smith had struggled his way across the continent, starting in his home state of Maine. From there, he followed the shifting frontier west, from one failed attempt at farming to the next. His final effort as a farmer ended in North Dakota after he lost an epic battle against a grasshopper (or locust) scourge. He abandoned his farm and headed for the Pacific Northwest, a place with plenty of rain and no locust invasions. He left his wife and possibly up to seven children, including a newborn baby, to try to establish a new life for his family. They remained on the residue of the North Dakota farm, scraping out an existence while they waited for him to send for them.

Smith's new job was to manage and distribute annuities and transform the Makahs into good Christians. His goal was to make sure that the Makahs could read and write in English, use English names and wear English clothes. Perhaps oblivious to the irony considering his own failures, he also wanted to transform the whaling and sealing tribe into good English farmers. His nickname was "Salvation Smith."

At the end of 1877, he finally sent word to his family to come to Neah Bay. As soon as they arrived, the entire family became ill with typhoid fever. On Christmas Day, their little girl Lizzie died of the fever. On top of that, Smith was fired from his job at the agency. He kept a detailed daily journal, but he did not explain why he was let go, although a few pages of his diary from that period were torn out.

As the surviving members of the Smith family fought to stay alive, Daniel Pullen showed up in Neah Bay on his schooner. Smith later wrote that Daniel was extraordinarily kind to the family, bringing them peaches, pineapples, beef and mutton and helping to nurse them back to health. One of Smith's daughters was eighteen-year-old Harriet, or Hattie. Although

Andrew Jackson Smith, La Push. Unknown photographer. *Bert Kellogg Collection of the North Olympic Library System.*

the typhoid fever had caused her lovely red hair to fall out, it's highly likely that this was when thirty-six-year-old bachelor Daniel Pullen first noticed her.

After many miserable weeks, the family finally began to recover. Mrs. Smith took the children on a steamer to Olympia and put them in school. A.J. stayed behind, accepting an invitation from Daniel to come to La Push and stay at his homestead. A.J. could check out the prime farmland that was there for the taking on what Daniel now called Pullen's Prairie. A.J. quickly staked a claim, apparently determined to try farming again. Over the ensuing months, he planted a large orchard of 450 apple trees, 300 plum trees and 15 cherry trees. He bought livestock and planted wheat and vegetables. Late that summer, with help from his neighbors, he built a log house for his family. And in September, he sent for them once again.

Meanwhile, Daniel Pullen had negotiated a contract with the Washington Fur Company to operate a trading post in La Push, which he opened in 1880. He brought in lumber to build the store and constructed a short railroad spur. The railroad was just long enough to allow him to transport deliveries from ships up the beach and into the trading post. That October, he left his homestead on "Pullen's Prairie," moved into a section of the new trading post building and opened for business. As part of the agreement with the Washington Fur Company that would prove important later on, Daniel was allowed to purchase goods from the store at cost plus freight.

According to A.J.'s diary, about 250 Quileutes lived in the village at the mouth of the Quillayute River at that time. He described fourteen long houses and fifteen "Boston-style" houses, with gardens producing potatoes and turnips.

Young Hattie Smith had taken a job as a teacher at the Makah agency school along with her brother Alanson Wesley Smith. Her tenure there was short-lived, however, and she soon joined her father in La Push. There, on February 23, 1881, she married Daniel Pullen and moved into his small apartment at the trading post. One year later, they had a daughter, Mildred.

La Push in the 1870s. Unknown photographer. *Bert Kellogg Collection of the North Olympic Library System.*

Daniel was a good catch. He was the richest man in western Clallam County. Bit by bit, he had increased his landholdings in the area by taking over the claims of relatives, friends and neighbors, as well as by bribing or threatening Quileutes to move aside. Homesteaders had to legitimize their claims by living on them and working the land, but Daniel lived at the trading post and paid some Quileutes to work his crop of potatoes. He got away with it because of their remote location and lack of enforcement. He also continued to build his reputation for bullying Quileutes out of their homes and for fighting with them during disputes at the trading post.

During this period, the latest Indian agent in Neah Bay became concerned that the Quileutes were not being educated in the white man's ways. Because there was no Quileute reservation, there was no Quileute Indian Agency and no Quileute Indian School. The Quileutes had refused to send their children all the way to Neah Bay for schooling. So, Hattie's brother Alanson Wesley Smith left Neah Bay and opened a new school in La Push. Daniel Pullen had previously claimed an empty house that was abandoned by a white pioneer. He proposed that the agency rent that building from him for the school, which it did.

Wesley immediately went to work renaming all his new Quileute students with English names, which he chose from his favorite political, biblical and

Alanson Wesley Smith. *Photo by Peterson & Bro., Photography, Seattle, Washington, Bert Kellogg Collection of the North Olympic Library System.*

familial figures. The children soon went home to their families with names such as Hudson, Lee, Cleveland, Taft, Penn, Washington, Jefferson, Jacob, Joseph, Esau, Isaac, Rebecca, Daniel, Mary, Martha, Mark, Bright (his future wife's name) and Pullen. One fellow was thereafter referred to as California.

Around the same time, a government surveyor came through to document the land around La Push. In his final report, he neglected to mention that the Quileutes had a village there. This omission boosted Daniel Pullen's contentious campaign to become a land baron. So far, no one had stopped him, and so he continued. Even when someone stood up to him, he seemed to win out in the end. On one occasion, he clashed with a powerful Quileute shaman known as Dr. Obi:

> *According to the version of the story recorded by* [Indian agent at Neah Bay, Charles] *Willoughby, Obi and Pullen fought over a fence that Pullen had put up. Obi apparently tore the fence down and, when Pullen confronted him, the Indian began hitting Pullen with a club and threatened to kill him until Clakishka, a Quileute leader, separated the two men.*
>
> *But, more than 60 years later, Obi's daughter recalled a different sequence of events, one that may seem more credible given Pullen's subsequent activities in La Push. Julia Obi Bennett Lee told anthropologist George A. Pettitt that Pullen had provoked the fight by trying to force Obi off Obi's land so Pullen could homestead it—something she said that Pullen had already done with other Indians at La Push. When Obi refused, Pullen grabbed Obi and the two began to struggle. As Obi's family members worked to separate the two, Obi picked up the club and began hitting Pullen. Obi was then arrested by his son, an Indian policeman in La Push, and spent most of the next year in jail, probably at Neah Bay.*[12]

In 1883, Daniel filed another claim on property at the mouth of the Quillayute River, right in the middle of the Quileute village. There, not far from the trading post, on a small hill with a spectacular view of James Island, he began building his Victorian mansion.

The following year, Daniel squabbled with his boss at the Washington Fur Company, who owned the trading post. This disagreement would later have critical consequences in the lives of the Pullen family. The man in charge of the fur company, Sutcliffe Baxter, claimed that Daniel had promised to sell him his La Push land and that Daniel backed out of their agreement. La Push had become more enticing in the eyes of potential investors—there was talk of a transportation hub for the maritime trade, including the creation of a big harbor. Some claimed that the railroad would soon arrive. The white settlers talked about finally forcing the Quileutes onto the Quinault Reservation. There would be a massive boom, and the cleverest players would get rich. Sutcliffe Baxter planned to be one of those players, but Daniel Pullen betrayed him and ruined his plans. As a matter of revenge, Baxter reported to the Indian agent at Neah Bay that Daniel Pullen was building a mansion in the middle of the Quileute village, on land that wasn't rightfully his. The Indian agent reported this information to the local land office, and it opened an investigation.

While Hattie Smith was caring for another baby, Daniel Dee Smith, born in 1885, both she and Daniel continued to operate the trading post. Her brother Alanson Wesley Smith was still teaching at the school. He had established an uneasy alliance with the Quileutes, despite the fact that the hated Daniel Pullen was his brother-in-law. During that period, an Indian agent named Oliver Wood wrote to Wesley, "The Quileute Indians are complaining bitterly against the action of Mr. Pullen, which I very much regret. They informed me that he demands a rental of them for the privilege of remaining at [La Push] and that he has ordered some of them to pull down their houses."[13]

In another letter, Wood wrote to Wesley, "California [a Quileute man] was here a few days since and complains that Daniel wants to tear down his house and then he refused to allow it done, whereupon Daniel beat and kicked him severely. Is there any truth in the statement?"[14]

Later, this altercation was apparently confirmed, possibly by Wesley Smith. Wood wrote an official annual report to the Commissioner of Indian Affairs:

> *Daniel Pullen made entry on the lands on which their village is located, and ever since that time he has tried to exercise full control of all the premises and endeavored to have the Indians pull down their houses for his accommodation....* [T]*he Indians make frequent complaints of the acts of Pullen, but as they are off the* [Makah] *reserve I am powerless to give them such protection as they should have. They have occupied this land*

> *from before the knowledge of the oldest Indian on the coast or any of their traditions. They have built some very comfortable frame houses and have several very large buildings built in Indian style from lumber manufactured by themselves, and they feel it would be a great hardship to be driven off and lose all their buildings and improvements, and all fair minded people will agree with me.*[15]

The report also quoted California's statement:

> *My house was removed…by Pullen; It was situated on the land where his house now stands. He came into my house and told me to tear it down; I said "No,…I have just finished a new house"…He came to my house again and sitting down by my side said, "I want you to tear your house down, I am going to build a house on this place where your house now stands. I want you to tear the house right off." I said, "No, Sir; I do not want to put my house off," and when I said "No" he struck me in the face and said "I want you to tear your house right off." I was holding two babies when Pullen struck me and I did not want to strike him back because one of my feet was cut with an axe and I had to walk around on crutches. I tore my house down; I was afraid of Pullen. He gave me a keg of nails.*[16]

In 1885, agent Oliver Wood left. The new agent, W.L. Powell, filed similar complaints to his superiors:

> *You will find several letters, written by the former agent here, on file in your office, about this man Pullen. He gives any amount of trouble and we can never have peace among the Indians there until he is removed.…It is a wonder to me that they have not killed this man, and if all I hear about him is true, I think they would be justified in doing so.…I have a delegation of some 20 Quileute Indians here, who have many complaints to make of their treatment.*[17]

Over the next few years, the complaints against Pullen continued, although it appears that the agency took little or no action to deal with him. In April 1886, agent Powell wrote to Wesley, "The delegation of Indians complain of Pullen making them leave the hill and come down on the beach where high tide reaches them. Is this so?"[18]

Despite these ongoing complaints, Daniel and Hattie finished building their mansion and moved in during the summer of 1887. Their fourth child,

Royal, was born that year. By then, authorities had assigned a special agent named Jay M. Carson to investigate the charges against Pullen. Carson reported that "Pullen has bulldozed the Indians so much that they have become afraid of him. This is how Daniel Pullen was able to file his La Push preemption claim without any problems. Otherwise, he would have been prevented from claiming all this land."[19]

Pullen also tricked a group of Quileutes into signing a petition that nominated him as their police chief. The petition was in English, and he told them that they were signing a petition to build a new road. The petition was debunked by Alanson Wesley Smith.

Finally, in October 1887, a few months after the Pullens moved into the giant mansion, investigator Carson's report brought results: the local land office declared that Pullen's land claims were fraudulent and directed them to be canceled.

If Pullen's enemies celebrated the order, the party was short-lived. The Pullens appealed. They stayed in their new mansion and continued life as before. The appeal took three years.

In February 1889, the U.S. government finally recognized the autonomy of the Quileute people. President Grover Cleveland signed an executive order withdrawing from sale and settlement eight hundred acres of land set apart for the permanent use and occupation of Quileute Indians. The new reservation encompassed most if not all of Daniel Pullen's land. However, the directive also indicated that it did not affect any "existing valid rights." Once again, the mixed message had the result of changing nothing. The Pullens stayed put and went on with their lives.

That same year, in September, most of the Quileutes left town for several weeks on their annual trip to pick hops for various farms in the Puget Sound region. On September 9, a fire flared up in the deserted Quileute village. When the fire finally burned itself out, the entire village was gone. As described on the Quileute Nation website: "[A]ll 26 houses at La Push were burned to the ground by a settler who had wrongly claimed the land. The fire devastated the last carved masks, baskets, hunting equipment and sacred regalia from pre-contact days, except for what may have been relocated to museums or private collections."[20]

Three months passed before a government investigator showed up and concluded that the fire had been an arson attack. Another new Indian agent in Neah Bay, John McGlinn, agreed with the general consensus that the arsonist was Daniel Pullen. McGlinn described the aftermath of the fire in his annual report to the commissioner of Indian affairs: "Mr. Pullen immediately planted grass on the site of the burnt homes and then built a barbed wire fence around the area five strands of barbed wire. This forced the Quileutes to rebuild their homes down on the beach which of course was subject to high tide."[21]

No one was ever charged. Several decades later, an anthropologist interviewed a Quileute man who was around twenty years old at the time of the fire. The man claimed that he witnessed Daniel Pullen and three others start the fire. In the 1930s, another Quileute, Harry Hobucket, claimed that Daniel Pullen had started the fire along with K.O. Erickson and Frank Balch, two other well-known settlers.

Pullen's aggressive behavior continued. He also made trouble for A.W. Smith and the school. First, he increased the rent on "his" building; then he served an eviction notice and tore it down. Smith asked a group of Quileute men to rebuild the school, and thirty of them volunteered and got it done. Meanwhile, Hattie Pullen had another new baby at home, a boy named Chester.

At the end of 1890, the government finally held a hearing about who owned the disputed land. Agent McGlinn argued for the Quileutes, saying that the Pullens should be removed. The local land office concurred and once again canceled Daniel Pullen's claims. Daniel appealed the latest decision once again, and this time he found a sympathetic ear in the commissioner of the General Land Office. It gave the land to Daniel Pullen. During the year of 1891, Daniel Pullen owned 1,500 acres in Quileute country, well beyond what any other settlers claimed and nearly twice the size of the reservation that the government had proposed.

The latest win in court boosted the confidence of the Pullens so much that they built an addition to the mansion, not only for their four children but also to run a boardinghouse. One of their boarders was a man named E.M. Williams, who lived in the Pullen boardinghouse for three months. Apparently to the surprise of the Pullens, that spring a colleague of Williams showed up unexpectedly in La Push—it was Sutcliff Baxter, the official from the Washington Fur Company and the owner of the trading post. Based on intelligence gathered by Williams, whom he had paid to live there and spy on the Pullens, Baxter charged the Pullens with stealing and fired them from the trading post.

On Tuesday, August 9, 1892, a sheriff banged on the door of the mansion with a summons. Both Daniel and Harriet were ordered to appear at the Superior Court of the State of Washington within twenty days to answer claims made by Sutcliff Baxter and the Washington Fur Company. Baxter had alleged that for the past six years, the Pullens had been stealing from the trading post to the tune of $18,704.51 (more than $600,000 in today's dollars). While the sheriff was on the premises, he confiscated ranching equipment and some of their livestock, including seven horses and a number of cows.

It took a year for the case to come to trial. During that period, each side gathered affidavits that supported their case. Baxter gathered twenty-three signatures from locals who signed a statement that the Pullens were bad people; some of these wrote additional notes. Even among the white settlers, there was considerable resentment, due to the ostentatious lifestyle of the Pullens and the fact that they had amassed a good ten times the acreage of anyone else.

Two of the affidavits were particularly notable. A dressmaker wrote that she had lived at the boardinghouse for several months and witnessed Hattie taking fabric and thread from the store. Another settler, John Carnes, stated that the Pullens did not farm or ranch their landholdings well enough to pay for their lavish lifestyle and that they must have been supplementing their income by stealing from the store.

When the trial finally began, the prosecution presented a case primarily against Hattie. She was grilled for seven days and answered more than four thousand questions. As an example, Baxter testified that Hattie had stolen two flamboyant hats that he had purchased in Seattle for sale at the trading post. He claimed that Hattie ended up with the hats, but the store accounts did not show her paying for them. On the stand, Hattie insisted that she had purchased the hats herself in Seattle.

After a monthlong trial and testimony from fifty-five witnesses, the jury returned a verdict of innocent.[22] Baxter motioned for a new trial, which was denied.

Despite this latest victory, the trial damaged the Pullens financially. The county tried to recoup the costs of the prolonged trial from Baxter, and he appealed to the state Supreme Court. All parties continued to pay hefty legal fees and travel costs to and from Seattle. To stay afloat, the Pullens had to mortgage their properties.

Even worse for them, the same week that they were acquitted of the theft charges, the Indian agent at Neah Bay wrote to them, demanding that they vacate their home and La Push properties within sixty days. The Department of the Interior had finally rendered a decision against them. Even though Pullen had adhered to the letter of the law, it said, his "deplorable and sometimes criminal behavior" toward the Quileutes outweighed other considerations.[23]

The Pullens sued for a restraining order against the agent who was responsible for throwing them out. That lawsuit delayed the eviction. It dragged on for several more years.

Nevertheless, the drama continued to drain them, both financially and emotionally. Although the details are sketchy, in August 1896, the pressure finally shattered the Pullen family. It's not clear whether the eviction was finally being enforced or if the financial ruin they were facing caused the rupture in the family. A brief newspaper article reported that "Daniel Pullen, a prominent farmer of La Push, Wash., suddenly became insane last Sunday and left his house and has not since been seen or heard of. It is believed he has committed suicide."[24]

It turned out that Daniel had not committed suicide and was still very much alive. However, something had sent him running from La Push and from his wife. He eventually made his way back to his old haunts in Port Gamble. There he once again took work as a bull puncher, although he was now a fifty-five-year-old man and almost completely deaf.

At that point, thirty-six-year-old Hattie made a bold move. She placed seven-year-old Chester with Dan's sister near La Push, and fifteen-year-old Mildred went off to boarding school in Ellensburg, Washington. The two older Pullen boys, Daniel and Royal, joined their father in Port Gamble. With only a few dollars in her pocket, she also abandoned their former life in La Push, including their great Victorian mansion. She headed alone to Skagway, Alaska, where she started over. Around that time, the Yukon Gold Rush was just gearing up, and Skagway was hopping. She immediately found work as a cook and moved into someone's abandoned shack. She began making extra money selling apple pies to hungry stampeders. She told people that she was a widow.

Hattie's apple pies put her on the threshold of an astonishing new career. By 1897, the entire family, including Dan, had joined her in Skagway. Daniel built another two-story house for the family, while Hattie continued to build her business. Despite Dan's efforts to remain as part of the family, their marriage was over, and he left by 1902. Later, he described himself during that period as "[t]horley brock up [*sic*]."[25]

The 1910 census lists Daniel Pullen, age sixty-seven and divorced, living with Alanson Wesley Smith's family as a "hired man." He became ill that year and went to Seattle, where he was nursed by his daughter Mildred. He died in August 1910 and is buried at the Quillayute Prairie Cemetery near La Push.

Harriet went on to become a famous figure in Skagway. In 1901, she leased a large stately mansion built by a Captain Moore (the original Skagway townsite owner). Two stories with a large dining room and big porch, the mansion made a perfect hotel, and Harriet had no trouble filling the rooms. She specialized in a "homey" atmosphere, likely filled with apple pies. She liked to entertain guests by dressing up as a Tlingit princess. She spun yarns about Skagway's early days and her encounters with the notorious con artist Soapy Smith. She earned the affectionate nickname "Ma Pullen" and rose to great prominence and wealth. The "Pullen House" was known far and wide in the region. On one occasion, the president of the United States, Warren G. Harding, showed up unexpectedly in Skagway and made a speech on the front steps of the Pullen House.

"Ma Pullen" ran the Pullen House for fifty years. She was the toast of society. She died in 1947 and is buried at Skagway. Her granddaughter continued to operate the house until the 1950s. Another descendant sold the place in 1966, but the property deteriorated until it was razed in 1990.

The Pullens' daughter Mildred married and divorced twice and had four children with her first husband. Two of the children were adopted by Ma Pullen. This caused a rift between mother and daughter—the former saying that her daughter had abandoned her children and the latter saying that her mother had stolen them. Mildred died in 1928 in Oregon and is buried near her father in La Push.

Pullen House, Skagway, Alaska. *Photo by Olaf Dale, Library of Congress, Prints and Photographs Division, Washington, D.C., 20540 USA.*

Their son Chester attended college in Washington. In 1912, he visited his mother in Alaska and died in a drowning accident on his way back. Their son Royal Pullen graduated from University of Washington, fought during World War I and became a mining engineer. Dan (or Dee) Pullen also went to the University of Washington and then to West Point. He became a football star there, serving as captain of the West Point team. After the war, he was awarded with the Distinguished Service Cross for heroic acts at Boi-de-Duisy, France. The French and Belgian governments also gave him honors. He died young of a brain tumor at thirty-eight.

As for the grand mansion that the Pullens built in the Quileute village, it became the office of the Indian agency, also known as the "Government

Opposite, top: Mrs. Pullen in Indian costume, Skagway, Alaska, circa 1926. *Library of Congress, Prints and Photographs Division, Washington, D.C., 20540 USA.*

Opposite, bottom: Members of the Smith family, Quillayute Prairie. *From left to right, back row*: Jennie Smith-Tyler, Oliver Smith, Harvey B. Smith and Mina (Minnie) Smith-Romeo. *From left to right, front row*: Alanson Wesley Smith, Mary Stewart Smith and Harriet Smith Pullen ("Ma" Pullen). *Bert Kellogg Collection of the North Olympic Library System.*

Above: "Government House," former Pullen mansion, La Push. *Photo by Fannie Taylor, Bert Kellogg Collection of the North Olympic Library System.*

House." Eventually, it was abandoned and began to deteriorate. In 1930, the U.S. government razed it as part of a plan to build a Coast Guard station. However, the station went up elsewhere on the reservation. The property where the mansion once stood eventually became home to the Quileute Tribal School.[26]

Chapter 3

SANCTUARY AT NEW DUNGENESS LIGHTHOUSE

1860s

If you wanted a stable life of hard work, fresh air and isolation, you couldn't do much better than taking up the post as keeper at the New Dungeness Lighthouse. In the United States during the early 1860s, the eastern half of the country was tangled in a brutal fight: the American Civil War. For William Henry Blake, a handsome and charismatic young man from England, serving in either army was not in the cards—either by choice or circumstance. The war was unlikely to reach the Olympic Peninsula, much less the New Dungeness Lighthouse. Or so it seemed.

During the summer of 1864, when the war had been grinding on for three horrendously bloody years, Blake was well established in his sixth year as keeper at New Dungeness Lighthouse. He must have been satisfied with his life there because he had already lasted a good deal longer than many lighthouse keepers did at such an arduous and secluded post. But Blake had found love and started a family. He and his wife shared the keeper's duties and cared for their toddler and a new baby. He had no reason to suspect that the Civil War would find its way to the far tip of Dungeness Spit. Or perhaps, if he had been following local politics, when it did, it didn't come as a surprise.

Blake is considered the first lighthouse keeper at New Dungeness; he began managing the lighthouse in February 1858, when the lighthouse had been in operation only a few months. Originally, twenty-one-year-old

Henry shared his lighthouse duties with eighteen-year-old Walter Blake, possibly his younger brother.

The keeper's life wasn't easy, particularly without running water or electricity. Periodically, a supply boat arrived, and the keepers unloaded the lighthouse's fuel supply along with life's necessities and carried these back to the station. Supplies included coal, lard oil, fresh water, food and other household needs. They hauled the lard oil (usually made from pork) ninety-three steps up the tower. There, the lard oil kept the light turning in its effort to guide passing ships away from "Shipwreck Spit." In addition to keeping the fuel supply steady, the keeper had to keep winding the clockwork mechanism that turned the light. In bad weather, particularly fog, the keeper also continuously rang the fog bell by hand. Someone had to keep watch on the water at all times, and it's likely that the keeper and assistant keeper worked in twelve-hour shifts.

Still, there was time to enjoy life. Henry had befriended a neighbor, Irishman Richard McDonnell, who with his wife and children had settled in 1860 on a farm near the mouth of today's McDonnell Creek (his namesake). Henry visited as often as he could and helped out when McDonnell fell ill. Unfortunately, McDonnell did not survive long on the farm; he died in February 1861. McDonnell was the first person to be buried at Dungeness Cemetery.

New Dungeness Lighthouse, Dungeness, Washington, late nineteenth to early twentieth century. *Bert Kellogg Collection of the North Olympic Library System.*

William Henry Blake. *Bert Kellogg Collection of the North Olympic Library System.*

Meanwhile, handsome young Henry Blake had fallen in love with beautiful eighteen-year-old Mary Ann McDonnell, Richard's daughter. The two married in August 1862, and Mary Ann joined Henry at the lighthouse keeper's house at the end of the spit. Henry also took in Richard's widow, also named Mary Ann, and her other children, including Richard Jr. (age eleven), Joseph (age three) and possibly including John (age twenty). The following year, the younger Mary Ann was appointed assistant lighthouse keeper, replacing Walter Blake. Henry and Mary Ann also started their family: their daughter Catherine was born in 1862, and their son Richard was born in 1864.

It was during the summer of 1864 that the Civil War arrived at the New Dungeness Lighthouse in the form of a terrified man being chased by a lynch mob. At the time, the keeper's house was crowded with the two families and a visitor, the customs inspector Mr. Brown.

The details about the lynch mob came to light later on when a local logging operator named Charles M. Bradshaw wrote an article about it for the *Washington Standard*.[27] Bradshaw, a former leader of the local Union political party, described how a "vigilance committee" consisting of Confederacy supporters had spent the previous spring doing everything it could to eliminate voters from the Union ticket in local elections. To do so, Bradshaw said, in May the men arrested a group of four Union voters, including a young farmer from England named John Tucker and another farmer named Nicholas Adams. The vigilance committee accused the men of being thieves and outlaws. The Union men were told to either leave the country or be hanged. The four men were then shipped off to Victoria, leaving their lives and property behind.

Months later, Bradshaw said, on the morning of the election, John Tucker came back to Bradshaw's place in Dungeness, intending to vote. Bradshaw convinced Tucker to go to Port Angeles, presumably to cast his vote in a location that was safer for him than Dungeness. However, a group of more than a dozen vigilantes, armed with rifles, found out Tucker had returned

Left: Richard McDonnell, namesake of McDonnell Creek and Henry Blake's father-in-law. *New Dungeness Light Station Association.*

Right: Mary McDonnell Blake, Henry's wife. *New Dungeness Light Station Association.*

from Canada and intercepted him. Tucker managed to escape the mob, but they chased him all the way out to the New Dungeness Lighthouse. There, possibly with Tucker hidden away somewhere, Blake somehow convinced them to give up and leave. They might have known that Tucker was there but perhaps were dissuaded by the presence of the two Mary Anns and the children. Either way, Blake and possibly Brown saved Tucker's life—for the time being anyway.

Meanwhile, according to Bradshaw, two of the other targeted Union men had managed to cast their votes in Port Angeles.

The following week, the Union men went to court in an effort to clear their names of the theft charges, which they claimed had been fabricated by the vigilance committee. They were all obliged to sell some property to pay off the court expenses. Once again, after they left Port Angeles and headed to Port Townsend, they were pursued by a group of six to eight men. During this chase, a storm moved in, and the Union men stopped for shelter with a Mr. Fleming, about halfway to Port Townsend. At Fleming's place, according to Bradshaw, the vigilantes caught up with them. They once again "arrested" the men, threatening to hang them unless they would "enter no suit against their persecutors, and not appear at court." In the end, the vigilantes took the Union men back to Victoria, British Columbia, and dumped them there.

However, John Tucker was having none of that. He returned once again to the United States, went to court and challenged the vigilantes to "bring their charges before the grand jury, if they had anything to charge him with." Bradshaw described what happened next:

> *No indictments were brought against* [Tucker], *and after Court he proposed to a number of men belonging to the vigilance committee to allow him to come* [to Dungeness] *and settle up his business, and he would leave them forever. They consented that he should come and do that, upon those conditions, and he came without any attempt at secrecy, and lived at my house until last Saturday, when an armed band of thirty or forty men came and surrounded my house and demanded admittance. I refused, when they attempted to open the gate by force, and I resisted but was soon overpowered. A number of them had their rifles leveled upon me, within two feet of my face. They then ransacked the house, searching apartments occupied by ladies, and frightening children out of their senses, but not finding Tucker as they expected. After stopping about the house a few hours, they left and nothing more has been seen of them.*
>
> *This morning Tucker took a scythe and went about a hundred and fifty yards from the house to commence mowing, and was shot in the back by some person secreted in the grass and behind a log, not more than forty feet from him. From the appearance of the grass there would seem to have been a number of men lying about in different places.*
>
> *This is the result of the acts of this self-styled vigilance committee. It was gotten up by men, all of whom voted the Democratic (pro-secession) ticket one year since, and for political purposes this year. They carried the election by means of it, and after using it for that purpose, would not let it drop without dipping their hands in the blood of their fellows. The county offices are all in the hands of men bound up in this pretended vigilance organization, and we can get no protection through the authorities.*
>
> *The Sheriff whose duty it is to disperse a mob, will do nothing, and we are to be bound hand and foot, one at a time, and shipped out of the country, or worse, we are to be shot down by assassins from every bush.*
>
> *Most of the men engaged in this committee are sympathizers with secession, some of them are lately from the South, and every man they have ordered out has been a firm Union man and a member of the Union*

> *party. Several of this committee are foreigners, having no right to vote, and refusing to declare their intentions to become citizens lest they would be liable to the draft.*
>
> *...This mob has, up to this time, had public sentiment in the adjoining counties in its favor, it is so easy to cry "Thief! Thief!" without stopping to prove it. But will it be in the future?*[28]

Bradshaw's account of the vigilance committee's lawless activity was later corroborated in a lawsuit filed in 1865 by one of the targeted Union men, Nicholas Adams. In his complaint, Adams names thirty-five defendants, including noted pioneers such as Elliott Cline, Harris N. McAlmond, Elijah McAlmond, John Bell and John Thornton. (Bradshaw, meanwhile, had become an attorney and was serving as Adams's lawyer.)

According to Adams's complaint, in May 1864, the defendants kidnapped Adams and carried him to the home of Elijah McAlmond in Dungeness, where they kept him captive overnight. The next day, they forcibly took him to Victoria on a schooner and dumped him there without money. Adams later made his way back to Washington Territory. He describes how he was at the home of Mr. (Matthew?) Fleming on June 12 when the mob arrived and kidnapped him. This time, they took him to the barn of G.H. Gerish and threatened to hang him. After three days, during which Adams begged for his life, the kidnappers voted to spare him. They put him in a canoe and dumped him once again in Victoria. They had so terrorized Adams, telling him that they would kill him if he ever returned to Clallam County, that he was forced to abandon his homestead. During the trial, the defense tried the brazen tactic of getting the case dismissed on the grounds that Adams no longer lived in the district. They also tried to argue that the statute of limitations had expired on the case. Adams won his lawsuit and was awarded $2,000 (about $40,000 today).[29]

There are no documents or family histories that provide insight into Henry Blake's politics or values. However, the fact that John Tucker chose to flee to the New Dungeness Lighthouse shows that he saw Blake as a sanctuary and perhaps his only chance to survive the lynch mob. The Tucker drama is not the only time Henry Blake and his family served as a refuge for someone in desperate trouble.

By the fall of 1868, Henry and Mary Ann Blake had been keeping the lighthouse for more than ten years, quite a long time. They had three young children: Catherine, Richard and Clara, all under the age of six. It's also likely that Mary Ann's mother, Mary Ann McDonnell, still lived and worked at the lighthouse, as well as possibly her son Richard, who was seventeen at the time, and her youngest son, Joseph, who was nine in 1868.

On the night of September 21, 1868, Dungeness Spit was choked with a heavy fog. A band of Tsimshian Indians was passing through the area, heading back home to Fort Simpson, a settlement on Prince Rupert Island, British Columbia. It was an extended family group of ten men, six women and two children, all traveling in one large canoe. They had been picking hops near Puyallup and had earned $500 or $600 for their efforts. They landed on the foggy beach and set up camp not far from the lighthouse.

It's not clear whether the residents of the lighthouse knew that they were there, but their presence had been observed by a group of Klallam Indians who lived in the area.[30]

A Klallam man named Lame Jack had been looking for revenge against the Tsimshians for kidnapping one of his wives and a son. Local tribal custom called either for payment or revenge for such an offense. The Tsimshians had not made any payment for the kidnapping.

Just before dawn, Lame Jack and sixteen other Klallam men attacked the camp. Historical accounts vary about the details of the violence and the aftermath, but what is known is that Lame Jack and the others slaughtered the entire party—or so they believed. The Klallam pillaged the camp and took everything. It was a significant haul. Historical records provided on the Jamestown S'Klallam website describe in detail what was taken: "One large canoe, five canoe sails, 16 paddles, seven buckets, three tin kettles, fifteen pounds of sugar, nine-and-a-half sacks of flour, one box of soap, eighty blankets, four trunks, six shawls, five calico dresses, four feather beds, two books, $330 in coin, one gold ring, one silver ring, five pairs of silver earrings, two pairs of silver bracelets, one large iron pot, one sack [of] clothes, four guns, one pistol, one pair of iron shaped hinges, and eight pillows."[31]

While this was all going on, a young Tsimshian woman named Chichtaalth lay still, playing dead. She was gravely injured, having been stabbed several times. She was also pregnant. According to the Jamestown S'Klallam account, after Lame Jack and his men had taken off, Chichtaalth somehow made her way to the New Dungeness Lighthouse. There the Blake family took her in and treated her injuries. When she was strong enough to be moved, the Blakes took her to Benjamin Rainie in Dungeness, whose wife was also Tsimshian. Mrs. Rainie had lost a half brother in the massacre, and Chichtaalth had also lost a brother. The Rainie family nursed Chichtaalth back to health over a period of six weeks, after which Chichtaalth made her way back home to Fort Simpson. Unfortunately, while Chichtaalth was recovering from her injuries, her husband in Victoria died from smallpox.

Meanwhile, charges were brought against the aggressors among the Klallam. Some accounts say that immediately after the massacre, several Klallams also killed Lame Jack. His compatriots apparently despised him, and they left his body on the spit along with the Tsimshian dead.

Either way, eleven Klallam men turned themselves in at the Skokomish Reservation, and the remaining six were hunted down and arrested. Most of them served four months of hard labor; others served longer. Any items from the loot that remained were returned to the Tsimshians.

More than fifty years after the massacre, a Tsimshian man visited the lighthouse. He spoke with the keeper at the time, Edward Brooks, and they had a conversation about the massacre. The man revealed to Brooks that the woman whom Henry Blake had saved that night was his mother, Chichtaalth, and that he was the unborn baby who survived the attack with his mother. Brooks let him know that Henry and Mary Ann's son Richard Blake lived nearby and that he had been a witness to the events. Brooks urged him to meet Richard Blake and perhaps to hear Richard's firsthand account, but Chichtaalth's son never did make the visit.

A few weeks after the massacre of the Tsimshians, in mid-October 1868, the barque (or bark) *Atlanta* crashed ashore on Dungeness Spit. The night was heavy with fog and smoke. The barque managed to extricate itself from the sand and sail on its way. When the captain, I.W. Snow, arrived in Bellingham, he apparently came under fire for some damage to the *Atlanta*. He blamed the lighthouse keeper for the incident, saying that the keepers had failed to blow the horn or ring any bell. He claimed that the keeper had seen him and only then rang the bell and that he could hear the keepers talking from his ship.

There is no record of a response from Henry Blake about the incident, except a letter from J.M. Watson asking for an investigation into the matter and saying that he had "always found Mr. Blake a faithful and reliable keeper." Watson signed himself "Comm. WSR Ins 13 LH District" (possibly insurance commissioner, Washington State Register, Light House District 13, of which New Dungeness Lighthouse was a part). No other records are available about any kind of investigation into the matter.

Four months later, in February 1869, the Blake family left the New Dungeness Lighthouse. A new keeper, Jacob J. Rodgers, arrived in February to take over, assisted by his wife, Esther Rodgers. Rodgers reported back to his superior that they had met with "hostility" when he told Blake to "turn over property." Again, there are no further records of this incident, and it's unclear whether he was referring to personal property on the site or the site itself or what exactly happened.

Either way, that same year, William Henry Blake soon had a new job—during the summer of 1869, he was sworn in as Clallam County sheriff. This new position for Blake may have indicated a shift in the political winds in Clallam County, perhaps away from the now-defeated Confederacy. Blake had come from County Kent in England by way of New York, and considering how he protected the "Union man" John Tucker, he was likely a Union man himself. During the time of John Tucker's murder, Charles Bradshaw had complained that the sheriff refused to do anything about the pro-secessionist vigilance committee. With Blake's election, perhaps that had changed.

It's not clear exactly how long Henry Blake served as sheriff; records do not exist as far back as that date. According to the 1870 census, the family was living in Port Townsend, and Henry, now thirty-three, was listed as working as a logger. Another child, Mary Ellen, had joined the family, listed as nine months old. Another child, Hannah, had been born during the interim but had died as a baby. Mary Ann McDonnell and her children were no longer living with the Blake family.

Unfortunately, sometime during this period, Henry came down with consumption, today commonly called tuberculosis. He died on May 5, 1871, in Port Townsend and was buried at the Masonic Cemetery, later renamed the Laurel Grove Cemetery. The Port Townsend *Weekly Argus* posted the following obituary:

> *Died. In this city, on the 5th inst., of consumption, W.H. Blake, native of Kent, England, aged 34 years. Boston papers please copy.*
>
> *Mr. Blake resided in this Territory since 1857, and was for twelve years light keeper at Dungeness. His funeral, which took place on Sunday, was more numerously attended than any that has occurred here before. A wife and four little children mourn for a loving husband and kind father.*[32]

The Masons also posted an obituary for Henry in the same column of the *Argus*, describing him as a "faithful and respected member…a true Mason…an esteemed citizen…a kind husband and father."[33]

Three years later, in the spring of 1874, the Blakes' youngest surviving child, five-year-old Mary Ellen, also died. Henry's widow, Mary Ann Blake, married their former neighbor, Edward Nathaniel Pilcher, on the day after Christmas of that same year, in New Dungeness. Mary Ann and Edward

Coast Guard cutter *Henry Blake*, May 22, 2019, in the Strait of Juan de Fuca. *U.S. Coast Guard, photo by Petty Officer Second Class Ryan Tippets.*

Pilcher had two children: Irma and Rachel. Mary Ann died at the age of thirty-five on November 29, 1879, and is buried at the Dungeness Cemetery.

A few months after Mary Ann's death, on February 29, 1880, the Blake's eldest child, Catherine Amelia Blake, married Frederick J. Ward of New Dungeness. That same year, the Blakes' two other surviving children, Richard and Clara (now orphans), continued living with Edward Pilcher, their stepfather. Also in the Edward Pilcher farmhouse were Mary McDonnell, age fifty-six, keeping house for Edward, and her twenty-year-old son, Joseph, listed as a laborer. By 1883, Richard and Clara had gone to live with their mother's brother, Richard McDonnell. The 1883 census shows Richard Blake, age seventeen, and Clara Blake, age fifteen, living in Dungeness with a farmer named Samuel Brooks, along with Richard McDonnell, age thirty-one; his wife, Laura (or Leora) McDonnell, age twenty; and their young children, Levi and Joseph.

In 1885, Richard Blake and Clara Blake, now nineteen and seventeen respectively, were living together in Port Angeles. Both later married and had families of their own.

On May 18, 2000, the U.S. Coast Guard commissioned the cutter *Henry Blake* in honor of the New Dungeness Lighthouse's first keeper.

Chapter 4

POMPEII OF THE OLYMPIC PENINSULA

1970

In the winter of 1969–70, a hiker exploring the outer coast of the Olympic Peninsula came upon a large mudslide near the beach. Among the mud and other forest debris from the fallen hillside, the hiker was shocked to detect numerous human-made artifacts, including perfectly preserved baskets and beams of wood. He spotted part of what looked like a house. And he was alarmed by something else: human scavengers.

To report this discovery, the hiker contacted the Makah tribe in nearby Neah Bay. The spot was located in the former Ozette Reservation, just south of Tskawahyah Island. Although the federal government had established a small separate Ozette Reservation in 1893, the Makahs had always considered the Ozette village to be part of the Makah land, and the Ozette Reservation was later dissolved.

Historical records indicate that the area had been occupied by a living village as late as the mid-nineteenth century. In 1834, several shipwrecked seamen from Japan had noted sixteen houses at the same spot. Five years later, a U.S. coastal survey agency that researched and managed a publication called the *Pacific Coast Pilot* reported a fishing, whaling and seal hunting village there with twenty houses.[34]

The Ozette village experienced a slow decrease in population as villagers moved closer to Neah Bay on the Makah Reservation. In 1920, the federal government required all American children to attend school. There was no school in Ozette, so families with children were obliged to move to Neah Bay. By 1937, the village had a population of one, a man named Fred Anderson—sometimes referred to as the last Ozette—who eventually moved to Neah Bay. The village, no longer maintained and exposed to the ferocious moods of the Pacific Ocean, eventually disappeared.

What the hiker came upon that winter day in 1970 were the preserved remnants of a much older village—one that had not been taken by the sea but rather had dwelt silently for centuries, untouched and protected beneath a mountain of mud.

Very few were surprised at the find. Makah oral histories described a cataclysm that had buried an ancient Ozette village hundreds of years earlier. Stories persisted about the lost village that was hidden below the thorny folds of the impermeable rainforest. It was commonly believed that the site had been occupied for several thousand years at least. Artifacts had been found, but the ancient Ozette village remained a legend—until the mudslide.

Back in Neah Bay, the hiker who contacted the Makah Tribal Council about the mudslide also warned them that people were out there stealing artifacts. The council chairman, Ed Claplanhoo, knew the hiker and had issues with the fellow, later referring to him as a "hippie schoolteacher" and a "dubious character."[35] It wasn't clear what area he was talking about. For that reason, Claplanhoo was skeptical.

Claplanhoo knew everyone in Neah Bay and knew everyone who owned artifacts. He'd heard of no problems. But the fellow persisted. The next Sunday, the same phone call. "Mr. Claplanhoo, they're still taking artifacts out of the house."

"So I said okay," says Claplanhoo. "I'll tell you what, you come to my house at seven o'clock tonight, and we'll talk about it."

The details Claplanhoo heard from the hippie schoolteacher finally got his attention. The "house" was not in Neah Bay, but at Ozette, at Cape Alava, twenty miles south of Neah Bay, reachable only by boat or a four-mile hike from the nearest road. Claplanhoo and the rest of the Makah Council decided to have a look. One of the councilors had a speedboat and the ocean was calm that day, so several members set off to see for themselves. They had orders to invoke the Antiquities Act if needed, a law designed to protect historical artifacts from scavengers.

Sure enough, they found pieces of an ancient village showing through the mud and debris of the fallen hillside. They also encountered people at the site, digging for artifacts. They evicted the scavengers, confiscated the items and hurried back to Neah Bay.

Village and shipwreck at Ozette, Washington, late nineteenth to early twentieth century. *Bert Kellogg Collection of the North Olympic Library System.*

Claplanhoo immediately phoned Dr. Richard Daugherty, an archaeologist at Washington State University in Pullman, Washington. Claplanhoo and Daugherty were both WSU graduates and had known each other since university. (Daugherty had been the freshman class advisor and Claplanhoo the class treasurer.)

Daugherty, who grew up in Aberdeen, knew immediately what they had found. Since his days as a graduate student, he had scoured sections of the Pacific coast for sites of possible archaeological interest, including the location of the Ozette site. During these research trips, he had identified up to fifty sites along the largely uninvestigated coastline of the Pacific Northwest. Of all those sites, he had considered Ozette to be the most extraordinary.

During these expeditions, he had found a few artifacts—cedar planks, basketry and whale bone. Based on these meager discoveries, he was convinced that there was something fabulous to find there. Unfortunately, he had trouble getting funding for any coastal sites. At the time, a number of West Coast dams were going up, and archaeological funds were rationed mainly to inland sites that would soon be flooded.

By the summer of 1966, four years before the mudslide, Daugherty and others had developed WSU into the "powerhouse of Northwest archaeology."[36] Their approach was multidisciplinary and included not just traditional archaeologists but also geologists, soil scientists and zoologists.

Petroglyphs at Wedding Rock, Cape Alava, near the Ozette site, 1954, apparently outlined in chalk. The boy is Jack Edward Zaccardo. *Bert Kellogg Collection of the North Olympic Library System.*

In the summer of 1967, three years before the mudslide, Daugherty secured the blessing of the Makah Tribal Council and a National Science Foundation grant to study the site. Daugherty and his students dug a trench perpendicular to the beach, 230 feet long, from the shoreline to the edge of the forest. One year later, they dug a second trench to the south. These diggings revealed a curious array of artifacts that pointed, at the very least, to a village of people engaged in seafaring trade with outsiders, including bits of metal, glass and firearms clearly from Euro-American sources, as well as Japanese coins. They also discovered a midden, or ancient refuse heap, that indicated inhabitants from at least 1,600 years ago. They were delighted to find bits of ancient rope, mats and baskets—all materials that would have disintegrated centuries earlier had they been even slightly exposed to the elements.

After two summers of work, patched together with meager financing, Daugherty was obliged to halt the excavation of the site. For the next few years, the archaeology department at WSU had to prioritize a separate discovery known as the Marmes rock shelter. The Marmes rock shelter was a cave discovered on the property of Roland Marmes at the confluence of the Snake and Palouse Rivers in Franklin County, southeastern Washington. The site had multiple sets of skeletal remains that were ten thousand years old, and it was at risk of being flooded by waters from the Lower Monumental Dam. At the time, the remains there were the oldest ever discovered in North America. (Although the Army Corps of Engineers built a levee to protect the Marmes site, water still made its way into the cave, and within three days after the Lower Monumental Dam went live, the cave was completely under water.)

Ozette landed back on the front burner with the February 1970 report of the mudslide. In addition to threats to the site from the looters, the winter weather on the outer coast was still raging and clawing away at the cliffs and exposed shoreline. Under the right conditions, between the wind, rain and waves, the weather could easily wash away the newly exposed site in a matter of hours. If that happened, an irreplaceable treasure of the western world would be lost.

A few days after Claplanhoo contacted Daugherty, they traveled to the site. In no time at all, they discovered whale and seal hunting tools, including a canoe paddle, halibut hooks made of wood and huge planks from a longhouse.

That spring, a group of Makah locals and WSU grad students, under Daugherty's tutelage, marked the beginning of a remarkable ten-year

Richard Daugherty (*left*) and Ed Claplanhoo assess the Ozette site and risk of continuing erosion. *Ruth Kirk, reprinted with permission of the University of Washington Press.*

journey that uncovered a uniquely preserved, centuries-old Ozette village that some came to call the Pompeii of the Olympic Peninsula.

The comparison is apt, although the village was encased in mud and clay instead of ash, as was often the case in Pompeii. It wasn't clear what caused the Ozette cataclysm, except that an entire cliff had abruptly collapsed and smothered the village. The coverage was so dense that the village was completely sealed off from decay-causing oxygen. Instead of hollowed-out impressions within hardened volcanic ash, as was the case in Pompeii, the household and hunting objects of everyday life from centuries before were still there. Even perishable items were preserved, including human beings who had died in their sleep.

Beneath the outer layer of mud and debris, the team encountered dense clay that required the use of water pressure to remove. The usual shovels and trowels were not appropriate for the site, so they set up pumps and hoses that brought water in from the ocean and sprayed the clay away from the delicate materials. The artifacts, many of which were wood or tree bark, began to deteriorate immediately as soon as they were exposed to air. These were placed into containers filled with polyethylene glycol, also known as carbowax, which served as a preservative.

As objects were removed, U.S. Marine Corps and Coast Guard helicopters joined the effort, airlifting the precious artifacts over to a lab in Neah Bay, where they could be cleaned and sorted. The bulk of the archaeological expertise was provided by Daugherty's team, while Makahs identified and explained the artifacts. The ancient Makahs had an expressive symbolic tradition and no written language until 1978. Only Makah elders could explain some of the numerous totems and pictographs.

Although this sudden bounty of ancient artifacts was a cultural boon for the Makah tribe, they had never stopped using their own language, preserving and singing family songs and honoring their traditional rituals and culture. For the archaeologists, the locals were a fountain of cultural and historical information; for the Makahs, the archaeologists shared the tools and methods of archaeology. For everyone, interest in Makah culture went into hyper-drive.

One archaeologist described the type of conversations that took place with the elders: "What did you use this for? What is this? That's a game. That's a paddle. The kids were playing games by where the fish were hanging and kept the birds away."[37]

When the excavation began, Daugherty set about raising funds, both for the dig and for a new museum to house the artifacts. He testified to Congressional committees and officials from government agencies. The U.S. government provided the initial $1.46 million to build the new museum, and other groups added funds to the project, including the National Endowment for the Arts (NEA), the Makah Tribal Council and the Crown Zellerbach Foundation, whose namesake has operated paper mills on the Olympic Peninsula.

The close collaboration between the Makah and Daugherty's team was exceedingly important to the project, and there would have been no excavation at all without it. Daugherty had grown up in Aberdeen and had developed a childhood fascination with archaeology while digging up buried objects on the beaches of Grays Harbor. Perhaps at least partly because of his local roots, he was determined not to make the same mistakes that characterized archaeology's spotty reputation during the past two centuries, where English, European or American scientists operated digs in other lands, pulling up everything and hauling it back home for a stunning display of someone else's history. Attitudes had changed since the seventh Earl of Elgin cut a magnificent chunk of marble façade from the Parthenon in Greece and put it on display in the British Museum.

For this dig, even back in the 1970s, all agreed, the treasures of the Ozette whaling village would remain with the Makahs rather than becoming the star exhibit of a big-city museum. As Daugherty explained, "A unique concept has emerged from the archaeological excavations at Ozette. It is customary that archaeological collections are removed to museums or universities, often remote from the location of their discovery. Because of the importance and richness of the material from Ozette, it is believed that it should remain at Neah Bay for the appreciation of the people whose cultural history it represents....[T]hese collections, properly displayed and interpreted, will be of inestimable worth in educating the succeeding generations of young Makah in their priceless cultural heritage."[38]

By all accounts, the Makahs and WSU teams worked well together. "Doc Daugherty," as the Makahs dubbed him, and his team trained Makah volunteers in the delicate art of handling and processing fragile artifacts. In return, Makah elders taught the ancient art of basket weaving to members of the WSU team. After the end of the excavation period, the Makah tribe managed the preservation, cataloguing and display of the artifacts.

During the eleven-year excavation, the site was occupied full-time rather than just during the summers. The wintertime staff was limited to around a dozen people, while they had as many as fifty-five workers during the summer. People who were there reported a great deal of camaraderie and focus, a family-like atmosphere. A fully functioning "village" rose up, with a water supply and twenty-four-hour electricity provided by a generator. They had a cook and a dining hall. Marine Corps and Coast Guard helicopters brought in supplies for the workers, in addition to their other duties airlifting artifacts back to the lab in Neah Bay.

The site was even open to the public—at least to those who could manage the four-mile hike from the road. Thousands came to see the archaeologists at work, including numerous Makahs who understandably felt a great deal of pride. Many had family members full of stories about the old Ozette, and others had relatives who once lived at Ozette. For them, the history was personal.

One critical fact that team members learned while living in the year-round camp was how the location worked in favor of the ancient whalers, even in winter. They had chosen their village site well. The southwesterly winds that dominated during wintertime were blocked to some extent by geological features, including a rock shelf that extended 1,800 feet into the swell.

Another defensive feature was Cannonball Island, a sea stack accessible by foot at low tide. It was an ideal location to process a whale, and whale bones were found throughout the site. In fact, whale bones accounted for three-quarters of the animal remains found on the site.

Ozette had been legendary as the best marine mammal hunting village on the outer coast. Traditionally, residents of other villages flocked to Ozette during the spring for the best hunting. Fur seals migrated through these waters, and every spring the gray whales came.

Scientists are still not certain when Ozette was buried. Some speculate that the date was around 1560; others say it's more likely that the great Cascadia earthquake of 1700 caused the hill to collapse. Daugherty believed that the site was four and a half centuries old, from the early 1500s. He later reported that some items had been carbon dated at two thousand years old. After digging deep below the buried village, they found evidence of yet another village beneath that one.[39] Multiple layers of civilization would not be too surprising in an area where endless storms add and subtract regularly to and from the coastline. It is a land alive with sea and wind, with king tides and mudslides, with ancient woodlands hiding the past, edged by wet, shifting landscapes.

Among those artifacts the archaeologists discovered from the past were the following: boxes, bowls, baskets, combs, looms, canoe paddles, woodworking tools (such as adzes, wedges, mauls and chisels), arrow flints, whetstones, fishnets, clubs, harpoon shafts and seal and whale bones for a coastal community that presumably relied on the sea for its subsistence. Remnants of imagery common to Indigenous cultures of the coastal Pacific Northwest—including thunderbirds, whales and wolves—were found inscribed on some of the walls and artifacts. This suggested that the people of Ozette shared belief systems, as well as artistic traditions, with coastal regional brethren such as the Tlingit, Haida or Kwakwaka'wakw.[40]

From the rubble of only three of the longhouses uncovered at Ozette, Daugherty and his wife, Ruth Kirk, documented an incredible number of artifacts:

> *40,000 structural remains varying from entire support posts and beams, wall planks, and roof planks to fragments as small as splinters; uncounted wood chips and other debris; a million animal and bird bones and shells; and 55,000 whole artifacts and pieces of artifacts…; catalog entries… enumerate 1,434 arrow shafts; 103 bows; 110 harpoon shafts; 629 halibut hooks and hook shanks; 324 canoe paddles; 840 wooden boxes;*

> *112 wooden bowls; 46 game paddles; 1,160 wedges; 579 whetstones; 30 iron blades (the metal probably from disabled ships that drifted across the Pacific from the Orient); 1,000 baskets (half of them intact); 80 tumplines* [a sling for carrying items on your back, with a strap across the forehead]*; 41 cedar-bark harpoon sheaths; 13 looms.*[41]

Daugherty said that "[m]ore than 400 wooden boxes, carved with figures of whales, seals and otters and filled with tool kits and food, were suspended from walls near sleeping platforms. In most [other] digs basket fragments are found. At Ozette more than 500 complete, perfectly preserved cedar bark baskets from the late 1400s and early 1500s have been recovered."[42]

The picture of life painted by the dig's contents was so comprehensive that the archaeologists were able to detect a difference in cleanliness between some of the longhouses. Daugherty surmised that the cleaner homes likely belonged to families who had slaves, which was common among the tribes of the Pacific Northwest.

The dig revealed the prominence of whaling and sealing among the Ozette, including "whaling harpoons, lances, bows, arrows, knives, adzes (short-handled hoe-like tools), house plants with carved figures of thunderbird gods, whales and wolves, intricately carved wooden clubs used in killing seals and carved heads of ceremonial clubs made of whale bone."[43]

The excavation teams and Makah experts believe that at the time of the cataclysm, about forty inhabitants lived in Ozette. In all, they uncovered the remnants of up to eight crushed longhouses made of great planks of western red cedar. The builders had used ropes made of bark and branches, along with huge whale bones, to build the infrastructure of the homes and to bolster outdoor waterways. Each of the longhouses was approximately 2,500 square feet (65 by 40 feet), with 10-foot-high ceilings and holes for smoke. Each longhouse had multiple rooms separated by low walls, with multiple families sharing a single house. Benches lined the inside walls in separate rooms, and one room was set aside for smoking salmon.

The numerous tools discovered in the gigantic haul of artifacts showed how they carved a living out of the harsh wilderness. For example, they built massive canoes out of cedar trees using cedar cutting tools made out of the bottom portion of spruce branches. Their carving knives were made sharp with beaver teeth embedded into the wood. Harpoon blades were made lethal with mussel shells and elkhorn barbs.

Their culture featured a high degree of artistry, as many of the artifacts were decorated with beautiful symbolic designs. Even the most mundane items were highly decorative. Daugherty speculated that the incredible abundance of resources, both from the sea and the rainforest, allowed the Makahs to establish stable villages and a reasonably prosperous life. They enjoyed enough leisure time to develop a sophisticated artistic tradition that is visible today throughout the Northwest coastal region, including its distinctive thunderbirds, ravens, eagles, bears and other symbolic figures. Elaborately decorated baskets are a still a specialty within the tribe, and several are today on display at the Smithsonian's National Museum of the American Indian.

Among the most unusual items discovered at Ozette is a blanket made of dog fur. Previous generations of Makahs bred a woolly haired dog, with a coat similar to dreadlocks, that lived exclusively on Tatoosh Island. These dogs were kept specifically for weaving blankets out of their fur. Back in the 1970s, some reported finding skeletons of the Makah dogs on the island; they are believed to be extinct today.

Daugherty said that the cataclysm apparently happened during the night when everyone was asleep. The human remains of Ozette ancestors were handled according to tradition by the Makahs and are not part of the public collection.

Excavation of the site ended in 1981, and it was then backfilled. Hikers visiting the spot may find some ancient petroglyphs carved on boulders, an abandoned ranger station or a memorial created by a Makah artist named Lance Wilkie, which reads:

> *From Osett endings have become beginnings. At Osett comes new understandings. Generation to generation our people have shared the wealth from the land and the sea. From this site we have gained appreciation of the wisdom of our forefathers. From this we gained new strength. In their honor we dedicate this memorial. This rich culture—our proud heritage. The Makah Indian Nation. Osett, Dia'th, Wa'atch, Tsoo-Yess, Ba'adah. The Five Original Villages Treaty 1855.*

More than eighty thousand artifacts from the site are kept, curated and displayed on the Makah Reservation at Neah Bay. Today, visitors can view many of the most spectacular pieces from the Ozette treasure at the Makah Cultural and Research Center Museum in Neah Bay. Among the most stunning artifacts is a large wooden replica of a whale fin covered with seven hundred sea otter teeth, a magnificent work of art that is totally unique. Experts said that this masterpiece may have been used in whale

Above: View of a memorial lodge built at the site by the late Makah artist Lance Wilkie, who worked at the excavation site. *Photo by J. Philip Gruen, 2017.*

Left: Plaque installed by Lance Wilkie inside the memorial lodge. *Photo by J. Philip Gruen, 2017.*

hunting ceremonies, which among the Makahs are elaborate and sacred, lasting many days.

Richard Daugherty described the Ozette site as "one of the most significant sites ever discovered in the Western Hemisphere." He explained, "Archaeological sites are labeled as being important for a variety of reasons, but no reason is more important than the completeness of the cultural record that has been preserved in the ground. In this respect, the Ozette site is unique for here are preserved not only the usual artifacts made of stone and bone, but also an almost complete inventory of the normally perishable items."[44]

Daugherty, who died in 2014, was married to noted outdoor writer and filmmaker Ruth Kirk. She wrote a book about the excavation and is also the author of *The Olympic Rain Forest: An Ecological Web* and many other books. Ed Claplanhoo, who was instrumental in establishing the Makah Cultural and Research Center in Neah Bay, died in 2010.

POSTSCRIPT: Ozette is not the only archaeological site on the Olympic Peninsula. A National Park Service document identifies a several other sites, some of which lie within the boundary of Olympic National Park. These include Deer Park, Hoko (at the mouth of the Hoko River); Manis (south of Sequim); Quilcene, White Rock and Sand Point (south of Ozette); Toleak Point (south of La Push); and Tongue Point (near the mouth of Salt Creek). Notably, another significant site was discovered in 2003: the Klallam village of Tse-whit-zen (pronounced ch-*wheet*-son), unearthed during a dry dock construction project at the Port Angeles waterfront by the base of Ediz Hook.

Chapter 5

VALLEY CREEK AND THE DESTRUCTION OF PORT ANGELES

1863

From the *Victoria Chronicle*:

> *A Dreadful Calamity.*
> *Destruction of the Town of Port Angeles*
> *By a Land Slide—Loss of Life.*
>
> *The beautiful little American town of Port Angeles (or Angels' Port), which is nestled at the foot of the loftiest spurs of the Cascade Range* [sic] *of Mountains in a direction nearly opposite to our own city of Victoria, has been nearly swept away by a torrent of water which burst upon it suddenly through a gorge or ravine which opens into the rear of the town.*
>
> *The calamity occurred about 6 o'clock on Wednesday evening last. The first intimation which the inhabitants had of the danger was a rushing, roaring sound, proceeding from the gorge, and on turning their eyes thitherward, they saw a great body of water, several feet in hight* [sic], *bearing upon its surface, or sweeping before it, logs trees and stumps, rushing down upon them. Before they could even realize their danger the flood was upon and over the greater part of the town. The customs house, a large, two-story structure, stood exactly in the path of the vast torrent, and was overturned and swept away in a moment. Of the three occupants in the customs house at the time, Dr. Gunn, the Collector, was the only one*

who escaped. His deputy, Mr. J. W. Anderson, and Captain Goodell, were overwhelmed with the building and lost their lives. Their bodies, mutilated and swollen, were recovered from the ruins after the water had subsided.

The flood next carried away the dwelling of Victor Smith (ex-collector), and his family narrowly escaped with their lives; and swept clear into the harbor the dwelling of Mr. E. Stanton, whose family were rescued with difficulty by boats. The front portion of the Rough and Ready Saloon, a portion of the wharf, and several thousand feet of logs were also swept into the sea.

Three or four miles behind the town, in fertile valleys several farmers have settled, and it is feared that they, too, have been overwhelmed by the flood. One of these farmers has a wife and four children with him. A person who visited the town on Saturday says that the picture of rain and desolation presented is indescribable. The fragments of houses, and hundreds of trees and stumps lie scattered in every direction, and in some places they are piled one upon another to the hight [sic] *of 30 feet. The face of the town site for a breadth of at least 100 yards by one mile long, is completely changed.*

The accident is supposed to have been caused by the late rains melting the snow and ice in the mountains, and causing avalanches into the lakes at the foot hills. These lakes were then overflowed and, rushing down the gorge, carried everything before them. It is said that the Indians told the whites, when they were laying out their town, that its site was subject to overflow, but no heed was paid to the information. By some, it is thought that the

Sketch of the original Port Angeles townsite in 1862, made by an unknown artist for a Canadian newspaper in Victoria. *Bert Kellogg Collection of the North Olympic Library System.*

> *customs house will be returned to Port Townsend, while others believe that the damage will be repaired, and that with proper care the recurrence of a calamity of the kind may be prevented.*[45]

At the time of the "dreadful calamity," on December 30, 1863, the settlement of Port Angeles had existed for less than two years. Its lofty status as U.S. Customs Port of Entry for the District of Puget Sound was even more recent—since September 1862. It was little more than a remote cluster of shacks thrown together at the edge of the Western world. For a nation entangled in an increasingly bloody Civil War on the other side of the continent, it didn't count for much. Still, its existence managed to garner the repeated, if distracted, attention of the president of the United States, Abraham Lincoln.

For the most part, this fragile outpost of white settlers—or at least the customshouse aspect of it—was the creation of a roguish booster named Victor Smith. An ambitious, bellicose man with a seemingly endless supply of grandiose plans, Smith had a figurative ace up his sleeve—his close association with President Lincoln's secretary of the treasury, Salmon P. Chase. His connection with Chase gave Smith an oversized influence and power that was equaled only by the incredible streak of very bad luck that afflicted the final years of his life.

Perhaps the greatest irony of the Valley Creek flood that smashed Victor Smith's dream was the audacious lengths he had gone to in order to make that dream a reality. In the process, Smith had earned more than a few enemies. The almost total destruction of the "first Port Angeles" probably inspired a good deal of raucous celebration in the saloons and offices of Port Townsend. The event may have also inspired some second thoughts on the part of his wife, Caroline (or Callie). Although her husband was out of town when it happened, she had been directly in the path of the flood and somehow managed to save the lives of her four young children, including a one-year-old baby. Some accounts say that she also rescued two others, including a woman who had been trapped under a log and was drowning when Caroline pulled her out.

According to Caroline's obituary, written in 1891, she was the first white woman to live in Port Angeles. (There were, however, at least several other white women in residence at the same time—all sisters of Victor Smith.) This "first" version of Port Angeles was less than two miles east of the ancient Klallam village of Tse-whit-zen, which was situated in a more secure location near the base of Ediz Hook. Radiocarbon dating suggests that the village of Tse-whit-zen had been inhabited for more than 2,700 years. It was one of many Klallam settlements along the coastal regions of what later came to be called the Olympic Peninsula. It's unknown how many people lived in Tse-whit-zen when white settlers began to arrive, but archaeological excavations begun in 2004 uncovered the remnants of six longhouses.

In the 1850s, only a few white settlers lived in the area, called at one point "False Dungeness," presumably having been mistaken for Dungeness Spit. Historical accounts name four bachelor settlers who arrived beginning in 1856 or 1857: Angus Johnson, Alexander Sampson, Rufus Holmes and William Windsor.

At that time, the Olympic Peninsula was part of the Oregon Territory, along with the rest of Washington and Idaho and parts of Montana and Wyoming. In 1850, two years after creating the Oregon Territory, the U.S. Congress passed the Donation Land Claim Act. The sole purpose of the act was to promote Euro-American settlement throughout the Oregon Territory. According to the law, each male citizen or soon-to-be citizen over age eighteen could claim 320 acres by homesteading there and farming for four years. (A dozen years later, Congress replaced the Donation Land Claim Act with the much broader Homestead Act, which opened up all territory in the western portion of the continent to settlers, although it was lowered from 320 to 160 acres.)

The sparse number of white settlers in "False Dungeness" effected a peaceful coexistence with the Klallams. One strange incident made its way into historical accounts. At the time, the Klallams and other tribes on the Olympic Peninsula buried their dead in canoes, baskets or other respectful containers. They often placed the container on a scaffold or in a tree and decorated it with the most treasured possessions of the deceased. As in European culture, special areas were set aside for these "mausoleums." One of the four settlers, Alexander Sampson, apparently didn't notice that his claim was in the middle of a large Klallam burial ground near Tse-whit-sen. The Klallams objected to his presence there and demanded that he move. After some tussling, the two sides managed to work something out without violence.

Eventually, the four bachelor settlers got together with some new arrivals and created the Cherbourg Land Company. They figured that there weren't any government officials around to make sure that they stuck to the terms of the Donation Land Claim Act—that is, the requirement that settlers farm their claim for a minimum of four years. Their intent was to file as many land claims as they could and then subdivide the claims and sell lots. Among the investors they drummed up for the Cherbourg Land Company were an

Ohio newspaper editor, Victor Smith, and the abolitionist governor of Ohio Salmon P. Chase.

Smith had been associate editor of a Cincinnati newspaper called the *Commercial*. As such, he had done a great deal to boost Salmon Chase's successful campaign for Ohio governor. When Lincoln was elected president in 1860 and appointed Chase as treasury secretary, one of Chase's first tasks was to appoint his good friend Victor Smith as customs collector for the Puget Sound District in Port Townsend.

On July 30, 1861, after a difficult journey from New York, Victor Smith and his family arrived in Port Townsend. The passage involved "an arduous trip by sea from New York to San Francisco with a crossing of the [Panamanian] isthmus by oxcart, another sea voyage to Portland, canoe and wagon up the Cowlitz corridor to Olympia, and now the ending of the journey's last leg, Olympia to Port Townsend."[46] At some point, Smith's father and several siblings also made the journey, apparently after he promised them jobs.

Victor and Caroline Smith were married in 1854 and had three very young children. During the journey, Caroline was pregnant with their fourth child. The young family settled at Fort Townsend, several miles away from Port Townsend, even though the military had recently abandoned the fort.

Smith's new job as customs collector was a powerful position. He controlled the hiring of customs inspectors, inspecting cargo ships and collecting tariffs on incoming merchant ships. He also managed the military hospital in Port Townsend and controlled the lighthouse service and revenue cutters (the precursor to the U.S. Coast Guard). The local revenue service had one cutter at Smith's disposal, named *Jefferson Davis* (a name bestowed long before the Civil War, which had erupted about three months before Smith's arrival).

The Port Townsend Customs House was a required stop for all ships entering the Puget Sound District. As such, it would have been the heartbeat of the city of Port Townsend, which had hosted it since 1854.

It's likely that Smith was unpopular in Port Townsend from the very beginning. He wasn't a local, and he secured his appointment through his nepotistic friendship with Chase. His background as a newspaperman served as a feeble qualification for the job of customs collector. As soon as he took up his new position, he set about removing any doubts about his predilection for nepotism by filling important positions with members of his family. He named his brother customs inspector. His father, George, became lighthouse keeper on Tatoosh Island and then later transferred to the new lighthouse on Ediz Hook. Two of Victor's sisters, Cynthia and Abby Smith, became assistant lighthouse keepers. Years later, Norman

Right: Secretary of the Treasury Salmon P. Chase. Brady's National Photographic Portrait Galleries, dated between 1860 and 1865. *Library of Congress, Prints and Photographs Division.*

Below: The first customshouse in Port Townsend (*on right*). The church on the hill is possibly St. Paul's Episcopal Church. *Bert Kellogg Collection of the North Olympic Library System.*

Original Ediz Hook lighthouse, built in 1865. Victor Smith's father, George Smith, and sisters, Cynthia and Abby, served as early lighthouse keepers. *Bert Kellogg Collection of the North Olympic Library System.*

Smith, Victor's son, described a harsh atmosphere within the Smith clan, writing in his memoirs about the violent treatment George Smith meted out to his dog and how all the Smith children hated "Aunt Cynthia" for her abusive treatment of them. This family dynamic could account for the way Victor Smith operated like a bulldozer.

Smith's political beliefs were unclear. His benefactor, Chase, was an ardent abolitionist, but Chase also had an uneven political history where he tended to jump from party to party. According to Norman Smith's memoir, his father was also an abolitionist. He wrote that Chase had instructed Smith to seek out and get rid of local "Copperheads," or "Peace Democrats," a group of anti-Lincoln Democrats who opposed the Civil War. Washington Territory had its share of Copperheads, including former governor Richard Gholson, who resigned the governorship on the day of Lincoln's inauguration. Gholson later died in Tennessee as a guerrilla fighter for the Confederacy.[47]

Norman's recollections, however, do not coincide with his father's actions in Port Townsend. Smith quickly took over a weekly Port Townsend magazine, *North-West*, after getting rid of its Lincoln-supporting editor by sending him

George Knight Smith, Victor Smith's father. He served as lighthouse keeper on Tatoosh Island in 1862 and was the first lighthouse keeper at Ediz Hook from 1864 to 1870. *Bert Kellogg Collection of the North Olympic Library System.*

on a fool's mission to Olympia. Once the editor was out of the way, Smith immediately began publishing antiwar articles.

More likely, it was Norman's mother, Caroline Smith, who held strong abolitionist beliefs. Caroline was born Caroline Rogers, daughter of the famous abolitionist Nathaniel Peabody Rogers. Editor of an influential antislavery newspaper in New England, *Herald of Freedom*, Nathaniel Rogers was a man ahead of his time, advocating for women's rights and animal rights. In 1840, he famously traveled to London to represent New Hampshire in the "World Anti-Slavery Convention." When the organization refused to seat female American delegates, he refused to participate. (However, Rogers does appear in a well-known painting of the convention that hangs in London's National Portrait Gallery).

Amid all his other activities upon taking up the customs collector office, Smith kept his focus on a singular goal: to move the customs port of entry from Port Townsend to what was then called "Cherbourg." He had a good reason for pushing the move: he wanted to increase the value of the growing number of land claims he owned in what would later be called Port Angeles.

As soon as officials in Port Townsend understood Smith's plans to move the customshouse, they went to work against him. On December 23, 1861, five months into Smith's tenure as customs collector, the House of Representatives for Washington Territory introduced a resolution *against* moving the port of entry to Port Angeles. However, the vote was postponed. Smith's enemies then escalated. "[O]n Feb. 10, 1862, a grand jury in Port Townsend indicted Smith for an editorial he wrote in which he charged that a resident had influenced an earlier grand jury. A judge dismissed the charges, writing that the jury had no authority over political appointees."[48]

Meanwhile, word of the squabbling reached Lincoln and Chase back in Washington, D.C., and they ordered him to report back to the Capitol. Before leaving on his journey, Smith appointed Lieutenant J.H. Merryman to assume temporary control of the customshouse in Port Townsend. This turned out to be a mistake. First of all, Merryman began auditing the books. He was shocked by what he found: "overdrawn $4,354.93 [more than $100,000 in today's dollars]; government funds deposited with private firms as security for personal loans; sale of the cutter *Jefferson Davis* was not credited to the government; a customs inspector was paid for a port trip not verified; a lighthouse keeper was paid less money than shown on the books; unqualified persons were treated at the marine hospital while qualified persons were denied treatment."[49]

But Smith's connection with Chase once again served him well. The charges were dismissed, and Smith not only kept his job, but on June 19, 1862, Congress also approved moving the port of entry to Port Angeles, effective September 1862. Furthermore, during his visit, Smith persuaded Chase to convince President Lincoln that he needed a federal reserve at the Port Angeles site. The reserve would be used for military, naval and lighthouse purposes.

In the end, Lincoln designated 3,520 acres at Port Angeles as a federal reserve. (Half a century later, in 1904, Port Angeles mayor Dr. Freeborn Stanton Lewis managed to get part of that reserve turned into a public park, today known as Lincoln Park.) The Army Corps of Engineers came along and platted a townsite on the reserve, which made it, in the eyes of some boosters, the "Second National City," after Washington, D.C., laid out by officials from the federal government. Just to keep Smith happy, the engineers modeled parts of the new town layout on Smith's hometown of Cincinnati, Ohio (including Vine and Race Streets, crossed by numbered streets).

In July, one month after Congress approved the move, a San Francisco newspaper, *The Bulletin*, arrived in Port Townsend with the mail. In the paper was an article describing how Victor Smith was in San Francisco, arranging for the cutter *Shubrick* to be transferred to Port Angeles, the new port of entry. His Port Townsend enemies readied themselves. When Smith arrived on the *Shubrick* in early August 1862, Port Townsend greeted him with a wall of resistance, not just from the townspeople but also from Mr. Merryman, who hastily hid away the customs records, locked up the customshouse and refused to let Smith enter.

In his book *The Last Wilderness*, the late historian Murray Morgan described the showdown:

> *Smith asked why.*
>
> *Merryman said Smith was a felon and an embezzler, that it had been his painful duty to write the report revealing that sad fact to their superiors.*
>
> *Oh that! Smith said he explained everything to Chase. Just a matter of bookkeeping. Merryman hadn't understood his accounting system, that was all period now the keys, please.*

U.S. revenue cutter *Shubrick. Library of Congress, Prints and Photographs Division.*

> *Merryman said he would await official confirmation of Smith's clearance before letting him back into the office.*
>
> *Smith turned and walked back to the* Shubrick. *From the saloons came the echo of laughter.*
>
> *An hour later Lieutenant Wilson, the skipper of the* Shubrick, *came to the customs house. He was a pleasant young man with a soft voice and a courteous manner. He said it was his unpleasant duty to tell Merryman that and on instructions from Collector Smith he had ordered his men to load the cutter's 12 pounders with double shot. They were at this moment trained on the customs house. If the records were not surrendered within 15 minutes, the bombardment would begin. It would be prudent of persons residing nearby to leave their houses.*
>
> *Merryman, after a quick consultation with the City Council, gave up the keys. A party from the* Shubrick *loaded up the records and carried them to the cutter, which at once cast off and moved out into the Bay.*[50]

While Smith was busy setting up his new customshouse in Port Angeles, a delegation of Port Townsend citizens went off to file a complaint in Olympia about Smith's threat to blow up Port Townsend. U.S. Commissioner Henry McGill issued warrants charging Smith and Wilson with "assault with intent to kill."[51]

A U.S. marshal traveled to Port Townsend, arriving just in time for the *Shubrick* to make another appearance in the harbor. The marshal boarded the *Shubrick* but did not find Smith on board. He read the warrant to Lieutenant Wilson, but Wilson refused to accept it. He cited a law that says you can't be served with a warrant on the deck of a government vessel. The marshal didn't know what to do. He went back to Port Townsend and contacted the commissioner, who said, "Yes, you can serve the warrant—go out and do it!" So he headed back out to the *Shubrick*, still at anchor in the harbor. But as the marshal approached, Wilson "ordered that the paddlewheels be started. They kicked up enough waves so that the rowboat could not approach."[52]

Two days later, the *Shubrick* dashed into Port Townsend at dawn, threw a line aboard the old cutter *Joe Lane* and towed it off in triumph to Port Angeles. Then the *Shubrick* disappeared. It was thought to have gone to San Francisco. When, in September, it was sighted approaching Port Townsend, a rumor swept the city that Smith had turned privateer and had come to sack the town. But the cutter churned past, going up the sound to Olympia, where Smith looked up the U.S. marshal and declared himself ready to explain everything.[53]

Smith's explanation apparently did not win over the territorial officials in Olympia, who soon assembled a grand jury. Forty men came to Olympia from Port Townsend to testify against him.

The cruise to Olympia took on some aspects of a community picnic. The passengers hung up a sign re-christening the sloop *Revenue Ship Number Two*. When they passed the *Shubrick*, anchored off Nisqually flats, they fired a derisive salute.[54]

The grand jury indicted Smith on thirteen counts involving charges of resisting a duly authorized officer, embezzlement of public funds, procuring false vouchers and assault on the people of Port Townsend.[55]

However, in what must have been another galling turn of events for Smith's enemies in Port Townsend, Smith's connections in Washington, D.C., once again cleared his name of all charges. The move to Port Angeles was complete. Smith moved his family there and built a house near today's intersection of Valley and Second Streets. He built a second building nearby that he rented to the government as a customshouse.

Meanwhile, in Port Townsend, his enemies constructed another case against him. They sent another series of complaints to Lincoln and Chase in Washington, D.C. Everyone seemed to understand that it was Chase protecting Smith. The *Washington Standard* newspaper at one point complained that Chase was always lax in releasing funds to support the state legislature for Washington Territory, while at the same time he had paid his collector of customs in Port Angeles, Victor Smith, four quarters' estimate in advance.[56]

The Washington surveyor-general Dr. Anson Henry was determined to get rid of Smith. He told Lincoln that Smith was not corrupt, but rather was "a swaggering, conceited egotist making himself offensive and odious to all" and "guilty of bad judgment and frivolous behavior." He insisted that Lincoln needed to fire Smith.[57]

Finally, Lincoln got fed up with all the drama and fired Smith. Chase was so loyal to Smith that he threatened to resign over the firing. The two men negotiated over Smith's fate and agreed on a compromise. Lincoln would remove Smith from the position of customs collector, but Chase could give Smith some other position to make up for it. So Chase gave Victor Smith the job of special agent of the Treasury Department assigned to Puget Sound.

Meanwhile, the customshouse continued operating at Port Angeles. However, during the summer of 1863, the stream that ran past the customshouse near Smith's residence, today known as Valley Creek, went dry. Apparently, nobody bothered to investigate the strange disappearance of water in the creek. Then, nearly six months later came the catastrophic December 30 flood that destroyed the town.

Later, it was determined that a landslide probably occurred somewhere upstream, perhaps high in the Olympics. A lake formed, which caused the stream to dry to a trickle. Finally, with the winter rains, the dam burst.

The flood hit the customshouse without warning, killing the two customs inspectors working there. Victor Smith—now a treasury agent—was out of town in Washington, D.C., but Caroline Smith and the children were in their home, directly in the path of the flood. Luckily for them, a logjam developed just upstream from the Smith home, and Caroline was able to get her children out safely.

In the aftermath of the destruction, a group of fishermen found the customshouse floating in the strait and towed what was left of it back to shore. A controversy soon erupted over a strongbox from the top floor of the customshouse that was said to be missing. Inside the box was $1,500 in legal tender notes and $7,500 in $20 gold pieces (approximately $205,000 total in current dollars). Henry Smith, Victor's brother, who was a lighthouse keeper on Tatoosh Island, heard a rumor that the strongbox was concealed in an "Indian village nearby." Officials arrested eight Klallams, and one was eventually convicted. Curiously, a story spread that the Klallams had burned the currency and the strongbox itself. The gold was never found.

The following year, the Smith family was visiting in the East when President Lincoln was assassinated. In May 1865, Victor, Caroline and the children left New York on a steamship, headed ultimately back to Port Angeles. During the journey, Smith and another treasury agent carried a large amount of currency that was to be delivered to the regional treasury in San Francisco. On May 29, 1865, the ship they traveled on, the *Golden Rule*, struck the Roncador Reef in the western Caribbean. All 535 passengers and 100 crew members managed to get off the sinking ship and paddle to a fifteen-acre island. The Smith family had purchased a number of household goods in New York to replace what they'd lost in the Valley Creek flood, and much of that was lost.

Ten days passed on the island, where the castaways survived on well water and water from a "condenser," along with whatever provisions the crew had saved from the ship—mostly salt meat and sea biscuit. Another passenger on the *Golden Rule* was frontier diarist Caroline Leighton, who wrote about her experiences in her book *West Coast Journeys*. She described the heat and the relentless sun during their days on the treeless island and how they tried to find cover by building walls using chunks of coral. For makeshift roofs, they used tattered bits of sail they salvaged from the *Golden Rule*, which was still stuck on the reef. She wrote that their fitful sleep was always disturbed by crabs nibbling on them.

A few crew members set out in small boats toward the small settlement of Aspinwall in Panama, a voyage of 250 miles. After ten days, two schooners full of turtle hunters arrived; they unloaded their turtles and took as many castaways as they could. A short time later, two U.S. government gunboats appeared.

Most of the castaways were taken to Panama, including Caroline Smith and her children. They journeyed across the isthmus and then boarded the steamship *America* for San Francisco. Victor Smith stayed behind, apparently alone, waiting for a revenue cutter to come and help him search the wreck for the treasury money. They waved goodbye to their father, and Norman Smith later wrote that this was the only time he had ever seen his mother faint. Several weeks passed while Smith waited, during which he contracted "Panama fever," or malaria. When a cutter finally arrived, crew members searched for the treasury safe in the ship's remains. They discovered the safe, but it was open and empty.

Two months later, Smith boarded another ship, a paddleboat called the *Brother Jonathan*, headed from San Francisco to Victoria, British Columbia. He was still very ill and "covered with boils, the result of exposure during the shipwreck, of being drenched with salt water and eating the hard tack soaked in salt water, beside the terrible tension of his helpless situation under the great responsibility resting on his shoulders. His friends urged him to stay in San Francisco until he had recovered his health."[58]

In the safe of the *Brother Jonathan* was yet another hoard of treasury bills, money to be used as payroll for U.S. troops stationed in the Pacific Northwest. The *Brother Jonathan* made it up the coast to Point St. George at Crescent City, California, where it smashed into a rock. This time, the damage was so ruinous that the crew could deploy only three lifeboats before the ship sank. Only 19 of 244 passengers survived. Among the dead was Victor Smith, who was still in his sickbed at the time of the collision.

Meanwhile, back in Port Angeles, Caroline and the children had moved into a house built by a man named Silas Goodwin, who had been paid by Victor to build the home while they were gone. They had bought yet another set of household goods in San Francisco, although a somewhat reduced supply. Their new house was located farther up a hill, east of the old customshouse. They had to cut a new road through the woods and haul their newly purchased household goods up to the house using an ox wagon or by dragging a sled. Norman reported that the children were overjoyed to be back home, with the "friendly Indians and the wild things, the fish and the clams, and oh, the freedom of going barefooted and bare headed!"[59]

After removing Victor Smith, President Lincoln had appointed Fred A. Wilson customs collector. Wilson was from Port Townsend, and he soon moved the customshouse back to Port Townsend. Although the platted lots from Victor Smith's federal reserve brainchild went up for sale in 1864, there was very little interest. Once the customshouse was moved, the washed-out town of Port Angeles went mostly to sleep. It stayed that way for another twenty-five years.

Meanwhile, Victor's widow now had a large family to support. They existed in a state of grief, isolation and financial instability. At the time of Victor's death, Caroline was again pregnant. The baby was born in the new house up the hill. One day after the birth of Victor Rogers Smith, the family discovered how poorly Mr. Godwin had built their new fireplace. It collapsed in on itself, and the house caught fire. At two o'clock in the morning, the family escaped through a window into the night. Fortunately, they had one nearby neighbor, a Mrs. Adams, who had helped with the baby's birth. They sought refuge with Mrs. Adams while their new home and all its new furnishings burned to the ground.

The family was then obliged to move in with the hated Aunt Cynthia, who continued her spiteful behavior toward the children. Finally, out of desperation, Caroline hired a carpenter to build a small house for the family out on Ediz Hook. Unfortunately, the equally unpleasant grandfather George Smith was the lighthouse keeper there, and his ongoing habit of stomping on his dog, Nero, deeply upset the children. The new house was also poorly built, and that winter, they had cracks in the walls and the ceiling that were big enough that their beds became covered with snow.

In her memoir, Caroline Leighton described the period of time she spent in Port Angeles. She painted a forlorn and moving picture of a "Mrs. S," a description that clearly refers to Caroline Smith:

> *Ediz Hook Light, Sept. 23, 1865. The light-house is at the end of a long narrow sand spit, known by the unpoetical name of Ediz Hook, which runs out for three miles into the Straits of Fuca, in a graceful curve, forming the bay of Port Angeles. Outside are the roaring surf and heavy swell of the sea; inside that slender arm, a safe shelter.*
>
> *In a desolate little house nearby, lives Mrs. S., whose husband was recently lost at sea. She is a woman who awakens my deepest wonder, from her being so able to dispense with all that most women depend on. She prefers still to live here (her husband's father keeps the light), and finds her company in her great organ. One of the last things her husband did was to order it for her, and it arrived after his death. I think the sailors must hear it as they pass the light, and wonder where the beautiful music comes from. There is something very soft and sweet in her voice and touch.*
>
> *Sometimes I see the four children out in the boat. The little girls are only four and six years old, yet they handle the oars with ease. As I look at their bare bright heads in the sunshine, they seem as pretty as pond-lilies. I feel as if they were as safe, they are so used to the water.*[60]

When winter ended, Caroline and the family moved into the abandoned customshouse on government property, which Victor had paid to have rebuilt. In 1867, Caroline had the building dismantled and reconstructed into a proper house on land that the family owned.

In 1869, Caroline married a local man named Lemuel Atkinson. The family headed east, settling in Iowa. Years later, when Norman Smith was in his early thirties, he returned to Port Angeles and made a name for himself, likely with considerable help from the land his father had claimed. Eventually, he became mayor. Caroline divorced Lemuel Atkinson and in 1890 joined Norman back in Port Angeles. She died in 1891.

Chapter 6

THE FAR-FLUNG BEECHER WHO MADE HIS MARK ON PORT TOWNSEND

1880s

Captain Herbert Foote Beecher stood on the deck of the *Idaho* and watched his men carry several hundred pounds of opium out of the ship's hold. It was Saturday night, the day after Christmas 1885, Port Townsend, Washington. Newly appointed collector of customs by President Grover Cleveland, Beecher was disappointed. He had expected to find a whole lot more opium on the *Idaho*—3,600 pounds to be exact. It would have been the biggest opium haul in the history of the United States. What he found instead of the other 3,300 pounds of opium were 500 barrels of oil and 400 tons of coal.

On Monday, he ordered his men to bore holes in the oil barrels and use a tool to poke around in search of opium tins. They dug around in the coal. At the end of these laborious and grimy searches, they came up empty-handed. Yes, they had caught several crew members with some contraband opium but had no evidence against the owners or captain of the ship. The major haul had eluded him.

Reluctantly, and probably angry and embarrassed, Beecher had no choice but to let the *Idaho* continue its journey to Portland. Beecher's disappointment, and subsequent resolve, might have been due to a need to live up to the renowned reputation of his illustrious family. Perhaps he felt it meant he really deserved the presidential appointment that was his at the young age of thirty-one, thanks to his famous father.

One thing was certain: Beecher intended to find out what went wrong. The previous month, a confidential informant in Victoria, British Columbia, had brought information into the U.S. consulate there about Captain James Carroll of the *Idaho* and his lucrative opium smuggling operation. The informant described how, during its next visit to Victoria, the *Idaho* would pick up 3,600 pounds of opium from the Tai Yuen opium factory in that city. The opium would come in half-pound tins packed into fourteen barrels and was destined ultimately for Port Townsend. Beecher had sent customs inspector Edwin Gardner to Victoria to investigate. Gardner and another detective had surveilled the factory and the *Idaho*'s entry into Victoria. They witnessed Captain Carroll meeting with the owner of the factory and later saw wagons delivering something in the dark to the ship.

The *Idaho* then set sail from Victoria. It followed its regular route north, through the inland passage to Alaska, where it would pick up other cargo before heading back south to Port Townsend. Beecher and his crew were waiting for them.

At the time of this operation, opium was still legal in both the United States and Canada, and Victoria was the center of the opium industry in North America. (It wasn't until 1908 and 1909 that Canada and the United States, respectively, outlawed the use and sale of opium.) In 1884, six Chinese-owned factories in Victoria processed raw opium into smoking opium and sold the highly addictive drug in tins or cans. By 1887, the number of opium processing factories in Victoria had risen to thirteen, which together produced more than ninety thousand pounds of opium every year. Those wanting to import opium into the United States had to pay heavy import duties, hence the rise of opium smugglers throughout the region.

The Chinese Exclusion Act of 1882 had made it difficult for Chinese to get into the United States, much less smuggle opium, so most of the black market was operated by white Canadians and Americans.

Although Beecher had let Captain Carroll and the *Idaho* sail off, he was not finished. He hired a diver to search the sea floor in an area known for opium dumping. The diver found nothing.

Beecher's persistence was equaled by his good luck. When the *Idaho* again returned to Port Townsend from its trip to Portland, Captain Carroll made the mistake of firing a seaman who had missed the ship's call during its previous visit. The sailor had been stuck in Port Townsend for the duration, waiting for the *Idaho*'s return. When Carroll refused to let him back on board, the man wanted revenge. He approached Customs Inspector Gardner with a story. The rest of the opium, he said, had been offloaded at a Kasaan Bay salmon fishery on Prince of Wales Island, Alaska.

Beecher realized that Captain Carroll had been tipped off about the original informant. He had hidden the opium before heading back south to Port Townsend. Beecher and Gardner decided to beat him at his own game. They could not contact the fishery in Kasaan Bay. There was no telegraph line to the settlement, and officials there may have been complicit in the smuggling scheme anyway. Beecher quickly requested the use of the U.S. revenue cutter *Oliver Wolcott*. They brought on a crew along with the vengeful seaman. Next they headed to Victoria to find a pilot who knew the inland waterways of British Columbia well enough to find a fast route north.

The *Idaho* was anchored at Victoria when they arrived. They were desperate to beat Captain Carroll back to Kasaan Bay, so after finding a pilot, they took off immediately. The *Wolcott* was not known as a particularly fast vessel, so they asked the new pilot to take them on the shortest route,

Port Townsend waterfront, 1891. The ship on the right is the U.S. revenue cutter *Oliver Wolcott*. *Bert Kellogg Collection of the North Olympic Library System.*

even though it was more dangerous. They sailed north for the 690-mile journey as fast as the *Wolcott* could go.

Captain James B. Moore was the *Wolcott*'s commanding officer. With the assistance of pilot Robert Hicks, they made good time until they headed right into a heavy storm. Despite the violent weather, they made it as far as Metlakatla, where they waited for eight hours to let the storm die down. Early the next morning, they pressed on. When they finally entered Kasaan Bay, they encountered a fresh obstacle: ice. The bay was partially iced over, and the open water was dotted with ice floes. They finally made it through without incident and found a spot to anchor. Beecher and a group of men rowed ashore to where the seaman remembered the barrels being offloaded.

The manager was absent, but the employees at the fishery assured them that the barrels were full of furs, as their labels indicated. The inspectors opened the barrels and found their prize: more than three thousand pounds of refined opium.

The victorious Beecher took the prize aboard the *Wolcott*, and they headed south for the four-day journey back to Port Townsend. They arrived on January 18, 1886, with their haul. It was indeed the largest opium seizure in U.S. history.

Herbert Foote Beecher had good cause to "feel justly proud of his feat," as described by the *Daily Colonist* in Victoria.[61] Married for four years with a two-year-old daughter at home, he had experienced several bumps in the road as he tried to find his footing in the world.

The youngest son of acclaimed abolitionist orator Henry Ward Beecher, Herbert had been educated at a private prep school and a seminary. Of his parents' eight children, four had died as babies or toddlers. The famous father was gone much of the time, and the marriage was said to be unhappy. There were rumors of infidelity on his father's part.

Herbert entered Amherst College in 1872 at age eighteen but left as a sophomore, ostensibly due to poor health. It's possible, however, that the real reason for his withdrawal was a widely reported scandal that had engulfed Henry Ward Beecher (and his whole family) that same year.

By the time the son Herbert was born in 1854, the father was already referred to as the "most famous man in America," due to his skill as a preacher and orator. Henry Ward Beecher had reshaped the stern Calvinist Christianity of his own prominent father, Lyman Beecher, into a more loving and open-minded system that promoted women's rights and fought against slavery. His sermons at Plymouth Church in Brooklyn were so popular that the crowded ferries from Manhattan to Brooklyn on Sundays were dubbed "Beecher Boats." His style was wild, colorful and humorous, with exaggerated gestures and rapturous storytelling. As his career developed, he injected his ideas into all of the big issues of the day and became sought after as speaker for a wide array of public events. He collected high fees for these speaking engagements. During the 1850s and '60s, he donated much of his money to purchase slaves, whom he freed. He also sent rifles to antislavery activists in "Bleeding Kansas," where a prelude to the coming Civil War was being fought on a smaller scale. The rifles earned the ironic nickname "Beecher's Bibles." He counted numerous famous Americans among his friends, including Walt Whitman, Henry David Thoreau, Mark Twain and Ralph Waldo Emerson.

But in 1872, the year that his son Herbert entered Amherst, he was accused of an adulterous affair with one of his married parishioners. The husband of the woman in question brought charges of "criminal conversation," and the result was a headline-grabbing trial that lasted six months and ended in a hung jury. Although he continued to preach at the same church and lecture widely, Henry Ward Beecher's reputation never recovered. The consensus was that the charges were true and that his paramour said as much in a letter to a newspaper. Nevertheless, when he died in 1887, fifty thousand people attended his funeral.

Reverend Henry Ward Beecher (*second from left*) and Mrs. Harriet Beecher Stowe (*second from right*), 1875. *Library of Congress, Prints and Photographs Division.*

Henry Ward was not the only famous member of the remarkable Beecher family, nor the only colossal presence overshadowing the life and ambition of young Herbert Beecher. Henry Ward's sister and Herbert's aunt, Harriet Beecher Stowe, had written what may be the most famous book in American literary history, *Uncle Tom's Cabin*. Released in 1852, the book was the first novel ever published that told a story from the perspective of a Black American. The protagonist is a slave named Tom whose owner sells him to a savage villain named Simon Legree. Tom's story had a massive impact on antebellum American society, portraying enslaved people as actual human beings—a novel concept at the time. The book sold 10,000 copies in its first week and 300,000 in its first year. Even more copies were sold abroad, including 1.5 million in Great Britain in one year. During the Civil War, Harriet Beecher Stowe met President Abraham Lincoln, who famously greeted her with the quip, "So you're the little woman who wrote the book that started this Great War." Today, the book is deemed by an international group of writers and scholars as number two on the list of most important literary works in history, second only to Homer's *Odyssey*. It has been translated into more than seventy languages.[62]

Like her brother Henry, Harriet had her detractors, and her famous work became fodder for unscrupulous producers and schemers. Within a few years of its publication, *Uncle Tom's Cabin* had been parodied and rebutted by proslavery writers, who cranked out at least thirty "anti-Tom" books. A series of plays called "Tom Shows" was created without her consent. These works employed stereotypes and caricatures played by white actors in blackface and featured absurd plots. The original Tom of the novel, a pious, forty-something Christian, became a shuffling, submissive old man. The Tom Shows were meant to be funny and entertaining for white audiences and left out the depravity of slavery. Other "Tom entrepreneurs" made a great deal of money off the novel by manufacturing household frippery called "Tomitudes," such as vases and butter dishes.

Harriet likely became a wealthy woman after the publication of her book. In three months, she is said to have earned $10,000 in royalties, which equals about $340,000 in current dollars. Her novel was quickly banned in the South, which somewhat limited its reach, but the only book to outsell it was the Bible.

Her brother Henry did not appear to enjoy a great deal of wealth, perhaps due to his penchant for giving it away. He did not keep his surviving children in fine houses and expensive clothes, but there was enough to offer a good education and to give them a boost when they needed it. Young Herbert had plenty of help, but in the end he had to find his own way.

In the years immediately after his father's trial, Herbert Beecher remained on the East Coast near his family. He worked with a steamer company and rose to the position of captain. Later, he briefly studied medicine in New York but withdrew from the program. In 1878, six years after his father's trial, Herbert headed west to California. He and a group of others purchased and operated a ranch for a time, but he ended up back at sea, eventually as a captain again, running steamers between Portland and Puget Sound.

In November 1881, he married a young artist, Harriet Bell Foster, in Seattle. He worked as captain of the *Otter*, a twenty-six-year-old steamship that sank in 1880 but had been raised and refurbished. He operated a route between Seattle and Tacoma. During this period, he also served as purser on the steamer *Idaho*, although it's not clear whether or not he served under Captain James Carroll of the later opium operation. Beecher was also reported to have leased the steamer *Biz*. In the summer of 1883, Beecher purchased two ships, the *Hope* and the *Evangel*, which implies that he had access to considerable funding, likely from the family. He continued running transport services, including mail delivery, until 1885, when he was given his appointment as collector of customs, which is when his troubles began.

In March 1885, Democrat Grover Cleveland took office as president of the United States. At that time, a number of Republicans, dubbed the "Mugwumps," abandoned their own party to support Cleveland, claiming that their party was too corrupt. Herbert's father, Henry Ward Beecher, was one of them. Ostensibly a Republican, which was originally the party of Lincoln and abolitionists, Beecher worked hard to help Cleveland get elected. One of his rewards was the appointment of his son as the collector of customs in Port Townsend.

The appointment was not popular, and Herbert Beecher quickly found himself the target of unfriendly comments. He was described as "dudish in dress and too airy in manner to suit the Jeffersonian simplicity of Port Townsend."[63]

It's likely that he hoped his success in capturing the huge opium haul, along with warding off another attempt to get the customshouse moved to Port Angeles, would gain him better acceptance and respect. But it was not to be.

His appointment by Cleveland had been made during a Congressional recess, and it remained to be confirmed by a Senate committee. In February 1886, shortly after the opium seizure, Herbert Beecher was called to Washington, D.C., for a hearing on the seizure and his confirmation as collector. A group of Washington Territory Democrats stood against him, and the confirmation stalled.

Another candidate for the post of customs collector reportedly dangled a $50,000 investment in Port Townsend for the position. Meanwhile, rumors began to circulate about "crooked transactions" that occurred when Beecher was pilot of the *Evangel*. In fact, Beecher was the target of multiple civil lawsuits in 1885, 1886 and 1887.

In April 1886, the source of vehement opposition to Herbert Beecher became clearer with an article published in the *Puget Sound Argus*:

> *The Beechers in Trouble.—There was considerable local buzzing this morning in town when the Oregonian arrived with the following among its associated press dispatches, under date of April 22nd at Washington: Rev. Henry Ward Beecher has been making some pretty severe remarks about the democratic party, much to the surprise of some gentlemen in that organization who thought that Henry was really and truly converted at the last presidential election. Beecher's son was appointed customs collector for Washington territory by President Cleveland* [a Democrat]. *Some time ago last summer the nomination was referred to the senate commerce committee, where it still remains. There is a great deal of opposition to the confirmation of young Captain Beecher, and it all arises out of a money transaction involving the small sum of $300. The case as laid before the commerce committee is that young Beecher was intrusted* [sic] *with $300 by a man who asked him to buy that amount of money orders. The man has never received either his money or his money orders. Beecher says he gave the money to a certain route agent, whom he is now unable to find. The route agent, however, has telegraphed Senator Dolph that he is ready and willing to swear that Beecher never gave him the money in question. The sub-committee has voted to make an adverse report.*
>
> *Henry Ward Beecher and Mrs. Beecher have both been here pleading with the committee, but to no avail....An adverse report from the committee probably means defeat of the confirmation. Capt. Beecher's main difficulty seems to be that the democrats don't want to confirm him because they want a straight out party man who would use the subordinate positions for democrats only; while the republicans would rather confirm a straight out democrat than a mugwump.*[64]

Apparently trapped in a political no-man's-land of partisan politics, Herbert Beecher spent the next few months fighting against the charges. The committee, instead of confirming his appointment, decided to investigate the charges, even though the amount of money was relatively small. Herbert, though still vehemently denying the charges, ended up paying Kepler the full amount in an effort to put an end to the matter. Despite these efforts, the committee did not recommend confirmation of his appointment. In the end, after paying $4,000 in legal fees to defend himself, Herbert Beecher lost the appointment.

In September, Beecher's troubles worsened. His notable achievement of the opium seizure turned into a morass of accusations. At the time, opium seized by the government was routinely sold off since it was only illegal if duties hadn't been paid. The *Evening Telegraph* in Tacoma, quoting an article in the *San Francisco Chronicle*, accused Beecher of embezzling $5,300 out of the sale of the opium. The paper also accused him of disappearing, using a headline on page one of "Where Is Beecher?"[65]

On September 15, the paper ran Beecher's statement in response to the charges:

> *The article from the Chronicle was "calculated to do me harm, and was started by certain parties for that express purpose....First—I desire to deny absolutely that there is any deficit of $5300 or any other amount of government funds in my position."*
>
> *He denied having disappeared, explained that he'd been visiting family in New York, then traveled back. He declared that his presence there could be verified by numerous prominent men in Washington, D.C., including President Cleveland. Signed Herbert R. Beecher, Late Collector of Customs District of Puget Sound.*[66]

It was clear that Herbert Beecher could count on at least one very important ally, and that was President Cleveland, apparently still indebted to Henry Ward Beecher for helping his election. In a move that eerily reflected the fortunes of the late Port Angeles booster Victor Smith, in January 1887 Cleveland appointed Beecher special agent of the Treasury Department for Oregon and Washington.[67]

Despite this latest appointment, the issue of missing opium money did not go away. Henry Ward Beecher died in March 1887 and was no longer there to help his son. In July 1887, the *San Francisco Chronicle* reported that a former deputy collector at Port Townsend named Abner Blake had collected a number of letters and affidavits testifying against Beecher. However, as Blake traveled to Washington, D.C., to present the documents, he died in Chicago "under mysterious circumstances."[68] Blake had been found unconscious at a Chicago train depot, suffering either from "concussion of the brain or narcotic poisoning." Blake later died, and the affidavits he carried somehow made their way into the hands of the *San Francisco Chronicle*.

Blake had been removed from the customs service, although the article did not say why or whether Beecher had anything to do with it. A source for the article accused Beecher of hiring a former seaman from the *Evangel* to murder Blake in Chicago. The source turned out to be the original informant in Victoria who had told Beecher about the opium being loaded onto the ship in the first place. This informant had been promised a reward for the intelligence—a percentage of the opium sale—but claimed that Beecher had cheated him out of the money.

Nothing became of these charges, and the *Puget Sound Argus* expressed some doubt about the matter, saying, "The *San Francisco Chronicle*'s attacks upon H.F. Beecher are very severe....[I]t seems to us that the evidence in the possession of the *Chronicle* is much too meagre to sustain the terrible charges made."[69]

The following year, Beecher's former inspector, K.A. Gardner, who took a large part in the opium seizure, was indicted for smuggling opium. Gardner pointed the finger at Beecher.[70]

Finally, that year, Beecher resigned his Cleveland appointment as special agent of the treasury for Port Townsend "by reason of a direct demand from the president." However, Cleveland's loyalty remained; Herbert continued as special agent of the treasury for San Francisco, although the family apparently remained in Port Townsend.

The *Seattle Post-Intelligencer*'s commentary on the situation seemed more an indictment of President Grover Cleveland than of Herbert Foote Beecher: "TO BE RID OF BEECHER. Herbert F. Beecher, special agent of the treasury department at Port Townsend, has been removed from this district to that of San Francisco....[T]he reign of the ring which has so long dominated the Port Townsend customs house is at last at an end."[71] The paper blasted his career as "striking commentary" of President Cleveland's administration.

In 1889, there was a further attempt to indict Herbert Beecher for extortion while in office and fraudulently moving public records: "It is very doubtful, however, if the indictments against Capt. Beecher will stand, as the period during which he is charged with having done these things happens to be the very time he was in Washington [D.C.]. He would make no statement to the Argus reporter as he had not been arrested."[72] Finally, according to the *Yakima Herald*, Beecher was indicted for "overcharging two vessels in 1886 of $5 and not accounting for the same to the government."[73]

Later that year, advertisements appeared in local papers for Herbert F. Beecher's new venture, the "Island Transportation Co." Beecher's new steamer, the *J.B. Libby*, made a weekly trip from Seattle, traveled among the islands, stopped in Port Townsend and went back to Seattle. Herbert's bad luck wasn't yet finished with him:

> *Sunday morning about 8 o'clock the steamer J.B. Libby, owned by Capt. H.F. Beecher, while about ten miles off Whidby Island, between Smith's Island and San Juan Island, in the Straits of Fuca, caught fire and burned to the water's edge. The passengers and crew were all saved. The vessel and cargo are a total loss, footing about $20,000. It had left the night before from Roche Harbor on San Juan Island, carrying 500 barrels of lime and produce, heading for Port Townsend. Bad weather sent her to shelter in a bay on Lopez Island, but she lost her rudder Sunday morning. She drifted toward Dungeness and they discovered a fire, caused by water slacking the lime. Captain White got seven passengers and crew of 14 on deck. They sent out distress signals, failed to get the fire out. They got into lifeboats. The four masted schooner, Jeanie, picked up everyone. They towed the burning steamer to Port Townsend. Beecher purchased her last April for $12,000 and put her on the island route. He had just added to his line the fine new steamer Point Arena.*[74]

Although Herbert Foote Beecher seemed to be cursed with a string of bad luck, his wife, Harriet Beecher, enjoyed much smoother sailing in her long career as an artist and teacher. She was known for opening the first art studio in Seattle on Commercial Street. There she gave lessons, mostly to society women, and she also taught art at the Territorial University of Washington.

After they moved to Port Townsend in 1883 and started their family, Harriet developed an interest in landscapes of the Olympic Peninsula, along with village scenes of the Makah and S'Klallam people. She opened a studio at the back of their home on Walker Street and resumed teaching. She received glowing notices in regional newspapers:

> *A most pleasing feature of the evening was the fine art exhibition from the art school of the college. This department has been built up by the efforts of Mrs. H.F. Beecher, a talented and accomplished artist, and an enthusiastic instructress. The oil paintings, water colors, and crayons exhibited included pieces by her pupils as well as her own work. Mrs. Beecher has the gold medal of the San Francisco Art school and is an artist of recognized ability.*[75]

Above: Captain Henry Foote Beecher and family. "Umma" and Harriet Foster Beecher are in back. Mary Eunice Beecher Susmann, Harold Beecher, Blanche Beecher (wife of Harold), Captain Beecher and Trixie are in front. The two boys are Paul and Sievers, sons of Hal and Blanche. *Collection of the Jefferson County Historical Society, #2005.91.7.*

Left: Portrait of Henry Foote Beecher by Harriet Foster Beecher, circa 1899. *Collection of the Jefferson County Historical Society, #2003.134.405.*

Above: The Beecher House on Walker Street in Port Townsend. *Collection of the Jefferson County Historical Society, #2005.1.1186.*

Left: Historic marker on the former Beecher House. *Photo by the author.*

In 1892, Harriet and her students accounted for 36 of the 150 paintings in the Washington State exhibit at the World's Fair in Chicago. Today, she enjoys a reputation as Washington's best turn-of-the-century artist. During her lifetime, it was said that she "brought art to the frontier." Tragically, she died in 1915 in a car accident. Herbert Foote Beecher died ten years later after suffering a fall from a faulty dock in Port Townsend.

Chapter 7

THE COPALIS GHOST FOREST

1700

> [A]*t a not a very remote period the water flowed from Neah Bay through the Waatch prairie* [southwest of Neah Bay], *and Cape Flattery was an Island. That the water receded and left Neah Bay dry for four days and became very warm. It then rose again without any swell or waves and submerged the whole of the cape and in fact the whole country except the mountains back of Clyoquot* [the west coast of Vancouver Island]. *As the water rose those who had canoes put their effects into them and floated off with the current which set strong to the north. Some drifted one way and some another and when the waters again resumed their accustomed level a portion of the tribe found themselves beyond Noothu* [Nootka] *where their descendants now reside and are known by the same name as the Makah or Quinaitchechat.*
>
> *Many canoes came down in the trees and were destroyed and numerous lives were lost. The same thing happened at Quillehuyte and a portion of that tribe went off either in canoes or by land and found the Chimahcum tribe at Port Townsend.*[76]

In 1864, noted explorer and western pioneer James Swan wrote these words in his diary after a Makah named Billy Balch related the story to him. Swan wrote further that he had no doubt that the story was true, that he had seen evidence on the Waatch Prairie "that the waters of the ocean once flowed through it."[77]

Swan's account is probably the earliest and most detailed written testimony about a gigantic upheaval occurring in the Pacific Northwest at some point during generations past. However, numerous other oral histories and creation stories describing flooding and earthquakes also appear from Indigenous tribes throughout the region, from Northern California to northern Vancouver Island.

The Hoh and Quileute tribes, who have lived for centuries along the west coast of the Olympic Peninsula, relate the story of an apocalyptic battle between two mythical figures of their pantheon: Thunderbird and Whale. Thunderbird was a monstrous bird who lived in a cave high in the Olympic mountains. Thunderbird wanted to catch and eat Whale, who lived in the sea. The details of the great battle include a great flood, shaking mountains and trees stripped bare and torn out by their roots.

In the early 1900s, a U.S. government agent assigned to the Quileute and Hoh tribes wrote down the story of the battle as it was related by tribal members. Later, a Quileute historian expanded on the written account:

> *"Thunderbird Fights Mimlos-Whale" (as told by Luke Hobucket). There was the great flood. At that time, Thunderbird fought with Mimlos-whale. The battle lasted a long time. For a long time the battle was undecided. Thunderbird in the air could not whip Mimlos-whale in the water. Thunderbird would seize Mimlos-whale in his talons and try to carry Mimlos-whale to his nest in the mountains. Mimlos-whale would get away. Again Thunderbird would seize him. Again Mimlos-whale would escape. The battle between them was terrible. The noise that Thunderbird made when he flapped his wings shook the mountains. They stripped the timber there. They tore the trees out by their roots. Then Mimlos-whale got away. Again Thunderbird caught Mimlos-whale. Again they fought a terrible battle in another place. All the trees there were torn out by their roots. Again Mimlos-whale escaped.*
>
> *Many times they fought thus. Each time Thunderbird caught Mimlos-whale there was a terrible battle, and all the trees in that place were uprooted. At last Mimlos-whale escaped to the deep ocean, and Thunderbird gave up the fight. That is why the killer whale still lives in the ocean today. In those places where Thunderbird and Mimlos-whale fought, to this day, no trees grow. Those places are the prairies on the Olympic Peninsula today.*[78]

Another Thunderbird story from the Quileute resembles the Makah story told by Billy Balch to James Swan:

> *"Thunderbird Causes a Flood." Thunderbird was very angry one time. He caused the ocean to rise. When the water began to cover things, the Quileute got into their boats. The waters rose for four days. They rose until the very tops of the mountains were covered with water. The Quileute in their boats sailed wherever the wind and currents carried them. They had no way to direct themselves. There was no sun. There was no land. For four days the water receded. But now the people were much scattered. When they reached land, some of the people were at Hoh; so they lived there from that time on. Others landed at Chemakum and stayed there. Only a few succeeded in finding their way back to Quileute.*[79]

The oral traditions plainly do not provide a time frame for this great destructive struggle for supremacy between land and sea. The best estimate is the vague "at not a very remote period," described by the Makah man Billy Balch. However, another source of corroborating information came to light in the late 1990s from almost five thousand miles across the Pacific Ocean, in Japan. There, a team of American and Japanese scientists identified historical archives that provide detailed descriptions of an "orphan tsunami," written contemporaneously by puzzled Japanese harbor masters and others. These documents not only confirm but also date the stories that came down from person to person among the tribes of the Pacific Northwest. They all point to the same thing: a massive earthquake and subsequent tsunami whose epicenter lay along a fault line that runs down the West Coast of North America, from Vancouver Island, down the outer coast of the Olympic Peninsula and Oregon, to as far south as Northern California.

In late January 1700, along the east coast of Japan, seawater from the Pacific unexpectedly inundated harbors and coastal towns, causing all sorts of problems. Japanese officials made inspections and documented the damage in detail. In a region that has always been all-too-familiar with earthquakes, nobody had reported one. Nevertheless, the tsunami damaged numerous homes, businesses and ships. At least four people were killed.

The waters drove villagers to high ground, damaged salt kilns and fishing shacks, drowned paddies and crops, ascended a castle moat, entered a government storehouse, washed away more than a dozen buildings and spread flames that consumed twenty more. Return flows contributed to a nautical accident that sank tons of rice and killed two sailors. Samurai magistrates issued rice to afflicted villagers and requested lumber for those left homeless.[80]

Numerous villages reported the mysterious floods at or around the same date and time of January 28, 1700.

In the town of Kuwagasaki, a harbor town on the northern shore of Japan's main island, a nighttime flood destroyed about one-tenth of the houses—thirteen were destroyed outright by water and another twenty burned in a resulting fire. At least one official who wrote about the sudden rise in seawater referred to the event as a tsunami. The damage was greater than any other tsunami in Kuwagasaki before or since, although no deaths were reported.

In Miyako Bay, a family in the village of Tsugaruishi kept a notebook that described a high-water incident in 1700 that destroyed homes along the shore in the bay, inundated other settlements in the alluvial plain and caused another fire that destroyed twenty-one homes. Those diarists also failed to feel an earthquake. Modern scientists estimate that the water rose along the shoreline as much as five meters.

The village of Otsuchi, thirty kilometers south of Kuwagasaki, was also inundated with seawater at the same time as its neighbor, damaging two houses and two salt-evaporation kilns and ruining nearby rice paddies.

The harbor town of Nakaminato reported the loss of two crew members and twenty-eight metric tons of rice that sank with the ship carrying it. The loss occurred when the receding tsunami waters collided with high waves generated by a local storm. The resulting watery turmoil pushed the ship onto rocks.

In the town of Miho, in central Japan near Tokyo, a headman described how the sea rose and fell repeatedly, like a "series of brief high tides," and again reported the curious absence of any earthquake.[81] Here, the tsunami was probably less than two meters in height.

Finally, in a town called Tanabe, located south of Osaka on the southwestern shore of the Japanese island, a castle moat was overcome with water and nearby farmland was flooded.

All of these carefully documented episodes occurred at the end of January 1700, at around a distance of 4,500 miles of Pacific Ocean away from the Olympic Peninsula. All were categorized as "unknown origin." However, in 1996, scientists finally connected the Japanese "floods" with the oral histories of Pacific Northwest tribes, and with tree ring dating that points at a massive Cascadia earthquake that took place between August 1699 and May 1700. The orphan tsunami of Japan had found its earthquake parent in the Pacific Northwest.

The Copalis ghost forest may have dropped as much as six feet during the earthquake. *Photo by Brian Atwater.*

Aerial view of the Copalis ghost forest. *Brian Atwater.*

Since making the connection, seismologists and geologists have found plenty of physical evidence on the Olympic Peninsula and elsewhere along the West Coast that indicates an earthquake above 9.0 on the Richter scale took place in late January 1700.

One such location is the ghost forest of Copalis. A few miles east of the mouth of the Copalis River, just north of Ocean City and Copalis Beach, Washington, the area is reachable via Plumb Lane or by watercraft. Three centuries ago, this was an old-growth forest of western red cedars and Sitka spruce. Today, it is a low-lying marsh dotted with dead and blackened stumps and tree trunks. They are the "ghosts" of the cedars, which are more rot-resistant than spruce trees. These ancient and twisted skeletons still stand three centuries after they died, while the spruce and other trees have vanished from the inundated area.

Using tree ring dating, scientists have determined that the cedars last lived during the growing season of 1699. By the end of 1700, at some time between September 1699 and May 1700, the trees were dead.[82] In other words, the annual addition of another tree ring stopped at 1699.

A short distance downstream from the ghost forest, in the hidden layers of sand and other material below the surface, seismologists have uncovered other evidence. There they found a layer of sand covering another layer of black peat that is webbed with tree roots. This indicates that the peat once had trees growing on it, and at some point it became covered with a thick layer of sand from the ocean, which killed the trees.

Today, the area is a permanent tidal marshland, inundated with salt water during high tide. The location of the peat layer choked with roots means that it was once a good number of feet higher in altitude, as much as six feet higher. Only a seafloor quake would create such a massive drop in dry land, and only a tsunami could put down such a layer of sand.

The ghost forest of Copalis is not the only "silent witness" to a millennia of seismic activity in the region. Another example is the tidal marsh at Discovery Bay near Port Townsend. The layers of mud and sand tell a story of at least nine tsunami deposits from as far back as 2,500 years. The closed-in physical setting of Discovery Bay grossly magnifies any tsunami action, and the marshy sediment tends to trap and preserve tsunami deposits. Of the multiple tsunami deposits that have been studied at Discovery Bay, several are assumed to be from earthquakes recorded elsewhere along the Pacific Ring of Fire. Those particular tsunamis in Discovery Bay were "orphan tsunamis."

Other deposits of peat and sand from the Discovery Bay site indicate a local earthquake. One of the layers studied by scientists (identified in their report as Bed 1) is a deposit of muddy fine sand of about ten centimeters thick, sandwiched between two layers of muddy peat. The scientists concluded that Bed 1 was likely caused by the 1700 earthquake.[83]

It took geological evidence and research on the Copalis ghost forest to give scientific corroboration to the oral traditions of a centuries-old cataclysm long circulated by the first inhabitants of the region. Together, these clues finally revealed the very existence of the Cascadia Subduction Zone, another major fault along the infamous "Pacific Ring of Fire." It is less famous than California's San Andreas Fault but potentially just as lethal. The team of American and Japanese scientists that uncovered the connection between the Indigenous narratives and the orphan tsunami felt in Japan have issued a warning in their report, titled "The Orphan Tsunami of 1700":

> *The fault that broke in 1700 has been reloading for future Cascadia earthquakes. If the fault behaves as it has the last few thousand years, the earthquakes will happen sporadically at intervals ranging from a few centuries to a millennium.... Sometimes the fault may break along its entire length; at other times it may break piecemeal.*
>
> *Today, public officials are taking steps to prepare coastal communities for Cascadia tsunamis, and engineers are using new seismic-hazard maps that allow for shaking from Cascadia earthquakes as large as magnitude 9....* [T]*he story of the orphan tsunami of 1700 continues through these public-safety efforts.*[84]

Chapter 8

THE BATTLE TO SAVE FORKS

1951

At seven o'clock in the morning on September 21, 1951, Art Anderson of Forks got up to the sound of rain on the roof. It had been one of the driest years on record, and rain was a very good thing—but it did not sound right. He stepped outside his home, and the heat hit him with a crack. It was raining, yes—raining burnt conifer needles.

His wife, Patricia, a former nurse, was pregnant and about to give birth. They hustled around the house and packed up the car with as much household treasure as they could fit. Then she drove away without her husband.

Art got into his wrecker and drove around town, sounding the alarm and getting a good look at what the editor of a Port Angeles newspaper later called a "living nightmare." "The sky has been so dark with smoke that no one can tell when daytime ended and night began," the editor, Earl Clark, wrote.

> *Fine ashes rained down from the sky in a ceaseless flow, filling eyes, hair, ears and mouths and coating everything in a fine powdery cover. There were only three kinds of sounds—the roar and crackle of the flames eating into the town, the scream of sirens as fire trucks careened through the empty streets and the urgent shouts of men's voices.*
>
> *Sparks and embers rained through the air, lighting on shingle roofs, in dead snags, in piles of kindling. Fanned by a strong east wind, which the heat of the fire generated into small whirlwinds, the embers set off hundreds of fires everywhere they lit.*[85]

Art and Patricia Anderson were not the first to raise the alarm. At three o'clock that morning, four miles northwest of Forks, Mickey Merchant, working the night shift as a fire lookout on Gunderson Mountain, had spotted a glowing red horizon. As he looked across the Sol Duc River Valley to the Calawah Ridge, what he saw was an out-of-control fire eighteen miles from the town of Forks. Although the smoke was thick, he knew that the wind was throwing the fire from tree to tree at a ferocious rate.

Immediately, he contacted John LeRoy MacDonald, the district warden for the state forestry division. In turn, MacDonald called urgent warnings to his contacts at local timber companies and the State of Washington. There were several very large logging operations in the area, including Merrill & Ring, Rayonier Inc. and Fibreboard Products. The forest service also ran logging operations, and there were smaller family outfits like the Brager family of Forks. Numerous sites were in the path of the fire. MacDonald then got to work rounding up as many firefighters and bulldozers as he could find. The town itself was in grave danger of burning.

At the Snider Ranger Station, a few miles north of the blaze, Ranger Sanford Floe also hurried to mobilize a fire crew. He and his eleven-year-old son, Sandy, helped evacuate a stranded family whose ranch was in the immediate path of the fire. Later, Sandy recalled the unusual hot, dry wind rushing up the valley from the northeast. He saw empty fifty-five-gallon steel oil drums galloping along the road on the wind. At six o'clock in the morning, Sandy and his father stopped on a road leading to the Kloshe Nanitch fire lookout and gazed out on a sight that Sanford later called the "saddest point in his long career." He understood that the blaze was moving far too fast on the wind and that any fire crew he directed into the path of the fire would be doomed. Any line of defense they could dig would have to be a whole lot closer to Forks.

It had been an uncommonly hot and dry summer that year—one of the driest on record. The Calawah Valley was parched; the river was dangerously low. As a matter of caution, forest officials had closed the Sol Duc River recreational area between July 2 and September 15 because of the fire danger. The entire Pacific Northwest region had been beset by fires.[86]

Six weeks earlier, on August 6, a fire broke out along the Port Angeles and Western Railroad right-of-way near Camp Creek, not far from Lake Crescent. On that day, shortly before noon, a steam-powered train hauling eighteen cars of logs and freight was headed east. The train crew was unaware that heat and sparks were igniting small fires along the tracks. They only noticed a problem when they pulled into a stop near Camp Creek to eat

View of the Sol Duc/Calawah Valley from the Knoshe Nanitch overlook. *Photo by Melissa Calloway.*

lunch and take on some water. As they ate, one of the crew spotted a small fire below one of the train cars. They rushed to back up the train out of the way and douse the fire. Satisfied that they had put the fire out, they got going again, heading east toward Port Angeles. However, at some point the crew noticed smoke where they had recently been. The conductor reported the smoke to Sanford Floe at the Snider Ranger Station. But Floe already knew about the fire, having been given a warning from another fire lookout. In fact, Floe had been told about more than one fire that had flared up along the railroad tracks.

At that time, the Port Angeles and Western Railroad was already in big trouble. Financial difficulties had forced cutbacks in operations, including safety measures. It no longer used speeder cars—small train cars that moved along tracks to check for needed repairs and other problems such as fires. It had also allowed its tracks and equipment to deteriorate. The tracks were overgrown with patches of vegetation, and old, rotting railroad ties lay scattered along the right-of-way without being cleared out.

By August 7, the next day, the main blaze was out of control. Floe had called in multiple crews. State and federal government agencies, along with the local logging companies and volunteers, battled the fire. Crews managed to lay down fire lanes, but the fire jumped them. On August 10, they finally brought the fire under control, after it had burned about 1,600 acres of forest. Over the next few weeks, spot fires persisted, and fire crews had to continue searching and tamping them down. Finally, by mid-September, officials agreed that there was no longer any sign of smoke. The August 6 fire was out.

Unfortunately, the fire was not out. A small patch of coal had simmered in a stump somewhere or in some other hidden spot. It was small enough to escape notice but ready to jump to life when an unusual hot wind rose up from the northeast. This is precisely what happened a week or so later, on September 21. The humidity had dropped drastically, and the northeast wind acted like a bellows on whatever had been left undetected from the August 6 fire. In no time at all, this second fire mushroomed into a full-blown blaze, gobbling up acres and acres of logging debris and huge piles of slash left uncleared and careening into untouched tree stands. By midmorning on that Friday, gale-force winds threw hot embers half a mile ahead of the main blaze. Burnt needles and even branches flew miles through the air and landed on rooftops in Forks itself. The main blaze made a direct dash down the dried-up Calawah Valley toward Forks.

Meanwhile, back in town, the 1,100 residents tried frantically to make life-changing decisions. Stay and fight the fire, and if so, how to do that? Evacuate? If so, what to bring and which way to go? One nine-year-old boy, Bob Henry, was told by his mother to choose one toy to save and bring with him. He was stupefied by such a terrible quandary—the teddy bear or the toy logging truck. His father yelled, "Come on! We need to get out of here! It's going to town!" Little Bob finally chose the teddy bear but also smuggled the logging truck in among the family's household goods.

Street scene, Forks, Washington, 1940s. *Bert Kellogg Collection of the North Olympic Library System.*

Twenty-year-old Lawrence Gaydeski was working at a logging site twelve miles south of Forks when the boss arrived at eight o'clock in the morning to warn them about the fire. At that point, the boss wasn't worried, but within an hour, the situation had changed drastically. Another logger named Bill Howard showed up and told them to bring their three tractors to Forks immediately and help dig the fire lines—right at the northern end of the town.

Soon, other fire crews showed up with flatbed trucks to help evacuate families and their belongings. Gaydeski got his family to safety, and then he and his son, Gary, hurried back to Forks to help his mother evacuate her restaurant, the Evergreen Café. She had just taken delivery of a huge supply of groceries for the restaurant, which Gaydeski hauled off to his own home on the Sol Duc River. After two of those trips, he went back to work on the fire lines.

Twenty-one-year-old truck driver Jim Mansfield rushed home from work and dug a trench around his own property. His wife, Pat, hurried over to the Forks Hospital, where they stripped beds, packed up and moved the patients to the hospital in Aberdeen, one hundred miles south. Then Pat and other women in town stayed to make sandwiches and coffee for the men digging the fire lines. Others watered down their homes and businesses with lawn hoses.

There was nothing but smoke and the crackling noise of the oncoming blaze and the sound of shouts. The street lights came on. The people hosed down buildings. They stamped out embers on the ground with their boots. They soaked gunnysacks and laid them on roofs. They patrolled the streets looking for sparks and embers. They looked for burnt needles flying around in the smoke and rushed to stamp them out.

Art Anderson spent the morning at his Kaiser-Frazer agency. Some of his cars were brand new; they still had paper around them. Terrified people came to him—they had no cars and could not evacuate. Art Anderson began handing out cars. He filled up each of the sprawling Kaiser automobiles with gas, handed over the keys and sent people on their way. Every single one of his cars was driven off into the smoke by desperate and grateful people. Maybe they would come back; maybe they wouldn't. If they did come back, none of them knew what they would find when they returned.

Some of them headed south to Kalaloch, and others headed all the way to safety in Aberdeen. Some tried to take 101 north to Port Angeles, but those folks saw the flames along the foothills, creeping closer and closer to 101. Soon the fire was burning alongside the highway. Later, it jumped 101, and the northern escape route was closed off.

At that time, Forks had two fire trucks and a simple water system that could muster only a fraction of water pressure compared to today's equipment. The fire department consisted of volunteers. Firefighters came from Port Angeles and Aberdeen and other towns with pump wagons. Two restaurants in town stayed open to feed them.

Within eight hours of starting, the fire had traveled eighteen miles along the valley, consuming everything in its path. At eleven o'clock in the morning, the fire reached the outskirts of Forks. Firefighters, policemen, loggers, businessmen, housewives, volunteers from Port Angeles and other Peninsula towns and people with bulldozers, boots, shovels and hoses were waiting for it.

The battle to save Forks was on. The fire created its own weather. Micro whirlwinds picked up pieces of moss and needles and bits of burned forest and sailed them into yards, onto roofs and along the streets. Where they landed, hundreds of small new fires started. Telephone lines were down. On the east edge of town, the fire jumped from burning trees onto barns and houses. The streams of water from booster tanks and trucks looked puny compared to the blaze. The heat was unbearable. Flames hit a group of bottled gas tanks, which blew up near a Port Angeles fireman, two hundred feet away. A barn at the outskirts of town exploded into flames, and then the farmhouse next to it burned. The fire consumed a group of tourist cabins, a house, a garage, a sawmill, a pile of cedar logs and a business. All along the outskirts of Forks, homes and businesses burned. The heat and the smoke and finally the flames threatened to kill everyone. The people were losing hope. The fire looked bigger and meaner than their courage.

At 2:00 p.m., fire officials concluded that Forks would be lost and called for mandatory evacuation. A sound truck drove around town blaring the warning over a loudspeaker to evacuate immediately.

And then something amazing happened. The hot, dry wind from the east abruptly eased and then shifted. From out of the west came a rush of moist ocean air that dampened the fire and pushed it away from Forks. Without the high winds from the northeast, the fire lost its ferocity, and the fire crews were able to get it under control.

That night, the town was quiet; 85 percent of the townsfolk had evacuated to safety, and the others prowled the streets with shovels, stamping out embers. The next day, a fire crew of 450 men remained in the area to clean up, search for spot fires and cut down smoldering trees.

A few days later, a mist crept over the town, and it began to rain, the kind of rain that Forks is famous for. The rain delivered the final death blow to the fire that almost destroyed Forks.

In the weeks, months and years that followed, the townspeople and local officials took stock. Fortunately, no one had been killed or seriously injured. The fire had burned thirty-three thousand acres. It burned federal timber worth about $1.5 million in 1951 dollars ($162 million today). That calculates to 600 million board feet of lumber. Numerous buildings, the sawmill and a lot of logging equipment were destroyed. A bridge was burned to nothing. The worst damage was at the north end of town, where Highway 101 enters Forks. Two dozen families were completely wiped out, losing their homes and everything in them. Others lost barns and garages, including trucks, equipment, tools and logs. One family lost their brand-new home and everything in it, including furniture, the washer and the refrigerator. Others lost their businesses. A tourist court was destroyed.

One by one, the people who had driven away in one of Art Anderson's new Kaiser automobiles came back and handed him the keys. He got back every single car. He also got a new son named Danny. It turned out that when Pat Anderson arrived at the Coast Guard station in La Push, she had gone into labor. The folks in La Push rushed her to the Quillayute Airport, where she got onto a Coast Guard helicopter that flew her to the hospital.

In December of that year, about twenty households and businesses in Forks sued the U.S. Forest Service, Fiberboard Products Inc. and the Port Angeles and Western Railroad company for their losses. Their complaint stated that the defendants should have properly put out the previous fire and that it had caused the fire that almost destroyed the town. Not surprisingly, the Port Angeles and Western Railroad filed for bankruptcy protection. The case went on for years, and in the end, the forest service was held liable for damages, having allowed the decrepit railroad to use the right-of-way through forest lands.

It turned out that much of the 600 million board feet of lumber was salvageable, and in January 1952, the forest service sold 425 million board feet of damaged federal timber. It was a much bigger sale than normal. Fire-damaged timber continued to flood the market for several years until it was all sold off at discount prices. The burn area was replanted.

Today, visitors can explore the Calawah River Valley and the old burn area by walking and biking along the beautiful Olympic Discovery Trail. There is no noticeable trace of the fire.

Chapter 9

THE LOST CHINESE COLONY OF PORT TOWNSEND

1880s

On February 7, 1886, a violent riot broke out in Seattle's Chinatown. The rioters were white workers, mostly union members, egged on by white labor organizers and other agitators such as the founder of the Puget Sound Cooperative Colony at Port Angeles, George Venable Smith. They demanded that Chinese workers be run out of town. At the time, Seattle's Chinese community was about 10 percent of the entire population of the city.

The mob forced about 950 people out of their homes and businesses. They rounded them up and herded them to the wharf. There they tried to force the people onto an anchored ship, but the ship's captain demanded fares. Someone came up with money to pay for passage, and the mob managed to expel a portion of the victims—a few hundred people. Local law enforcement arrived and tried to break up the rabble. They tried to protect the remaining Chinese and escort them back to their homes. Some people within the mob battled the police. In the ensuing violence, one man was killed and five others were injured.

Authorities declared martial law, which lasted for two weeks. They promised the remaining Chinese protection, but many chose to leave anyway. Some of those leaving, almost one hundred people, headed to a nearby town that was said to be less hostile to Chinese people—Port Townsend.

Port Townsend's reputation as a safe haven was only partially true. Its remote location and smaller population seemed to protect it from the worst of the racist fervor emanating from Seattle and Tacoma, but there was still plenty of anti-Chinese sentiment in the port city. The local press continuously reprinted inflammatory articles from other newspapers. As in other towns, white labor leaders in Port Townsend complained that there were too many Chinese. White union members resented the Chinese for being more compliant about accepting low wages and tolerating bad working conditions. The cheap Chinese labor undercut the power of the unions. In a situation that worked well for the captains of industry, the two labor pools were separated by a deep language and cultural schism. Chinese workers did not tend to join white labor unions.

In 1885, the local Knights of Labor demanded that the Port Townsend mill company get rid of its Chinese employees and replace them with whites. The firm gave in, and the Knights of Labor then went to work on other mills. The *Port Townsend Argos* successfully called for a boycott of the Chinese and their employers.

However, the boycott was short-lived. One brickmaker who employed Chinese workers warned everyone that the price of bricks was going to go way up. The companies that had given in to the Knights of Labor and *Argos* demands slowly began rehiring their Chinese workers. Three years later, another petition went around to do the same; this time the *Argos* was against it.

One common argument against the Chinese was that they didn't contribute to the community because they sent their earnings home to China. However, in the case of Port Townsend, they often invested their earnings locally. They put their money in the town's banks. The Merchants Bank in town had a special teller window for the Chinese. Some bought real estate until they were forbidden to do so in the state constitution in 1889. After that, they continued to lease acreage.

Fortunately, Port Townsend had seen very little of the violence that other cities saw, and when attacks occurred, members of the local Chinese community tended to fight back. There were a few incidents of vandalism and assaults. One white man attacked a Chinese man and dragged him around by his queue. Unlike in other cities, the Chinese community in Port Townsend took the assailant to court for assault. Another Chinese victim knocked out his attacker, reportedly to the applause of the crowd. Yet another Chinese man was attacked with a rock and returned later with a gun, which others had to wrestle away from him.

In fact, unlike in other towns and cities, the Chinese colony of Port Townsend played a significant role in the business development of the town, despite the relatively small number of Chinese residents. In the 1871 territorial census, the total population of Jefferson County was 1,200, with only 21 Chinese. By 1890, the Chinese population peaked at 453 out of a total of 8,368 people in Port Townsend, about 5 percent of the population. The increase was likely due at least partly to the influx of refugees from the riot in Seattle and another riot that took place in Tacoma in 1885.

It's likely that additional Chinese were hiding from census workers, but in general the Chinese percent of the population always remained small. Almost all of them were male. In 1880, the census reported six female Chinese residents. Two were the wives of merchants, two were daughters of merchants and two were prostitutes.

One could argue that a primary reason for the relative influence and security of the Port Townsend Chinese community was down to one man, named Ng Soon. In 1885, one year before the Seattle riot, the largest business in Port Townsend was the Zee Tai Company, owned by Ng Soon. He had established his company in 1879, with a modest beginning as a small shop. By 1889, he had moved to 300 Water Street. (Today, the old Zee Tai building is at 816 Water Street.) The store sold Asian goods imported from China, including tea, rice and opium. In 1889, Zee Tai reported a gross profit of $100,000, about $3.3 million in today's dollars.

Ng Soon was a clever businessman and spoke good English. He enjoyed a good reputation in town. It is likely that it was his presence in Port Townsend that gave the town its image as a safe place to land for the Chinese residents who had been run out of Seattle.

Ng Soon and other Chinese businessmen in Port Townsend took the Chinese Exclusion Act of 1882 in stride. The act blocked Chinese laborers from entering the country for a period of ten years, but Chinese merchants were welcomed. Hence, many of the Chinese businesses in Port Townsend had numerous "partners." For example, the Yet Wo Company had ten partners, each with the status of "merchant." However, Yet Wo only had $300 in merchandise. Another business, the Get Kee company, had twenty partners but only a three-hundred-square-foot store. It's likely that the majority of "partners" in these companies were actually laborers.

Typical Chinese businesses did a lot more than sell goods. They doubled as the local Chinese social club. They hosted gambling and opium dens. Many also provided immigration, housing and job referral services. In an interview with the Jefferson County Historical Society, a descendant named

The Zee Tai building is shown at the center (large black sign with white lettering on the side and long extension at the back). Port Townsend, Union Wharf, 1889. *Collection of the Jefferson County Historical Society, #2004.117.519.*

Long Fannie Lung described her childhood in Port Townsend's Chinatown as the daughter of a merchant. She said that new Chinese immigrants came regularly through her father's store.

The Zee Tai Company's operation went far beyond providing Chinese goods to Port Townsend customers. The company operated as a job service for Chinese laborers, serving local employers such as mills and canneries. Zee Tai reportedly supplied cannery workers all along the western coast, from Portland to Alaska. As payment for finding a job for the worker, a broker such as Zee Tai did not take a percentage of wages, as current-day staffing agencies do; instead, they sold supplies to and provided housing for monthly fees.

Another typical business for the Port Townsend Chinese community was providing laundry services. Chinese laundries generally enjoyed a good reputation, but they came under scrutiny in town for dumping washwater outdoors and creating an environmental nuisance. The city imposed a fee of twenty dollars per year exclusively on Chinese laundries, although all laundries were guilty of doing the same. The Chinese answered by raising their prices and successfully challenged the ordinance.

The Chinatown area of Port Townsend existed mainly along the waterfront between Washington and Water Streets and between Adams and Madison Streets in today's downtown. At the time, at least part of this area was tidal flats, and the homes were sometimes built on pilings.

Above: Today a popular open space for outdoor recreation, the Chinese Gardens were cleared and managed by immigrant Chinese gardeners as a communal business. It was located at the northwest edge of Fort Worden State Park. *Photo by the author.*

Left: Sign with map of the former Chinese Gardens of Port Townsend. *Photo by the author.*

Local Chinese entrepreneurs also leased acreage outside of town to grow vegetables. Today, the acreage is an open space near North Beach, still known as the Chinese Gardens. The industrious gardeners banded together and leased this land for a large community garden. They built a tide gate that kept seawater out at high tide but allowed excess rainwater to drain.

The collective gardeners, known as truck gardeners, sold their produce door to door. They also leased a barn in Port Townsend to use as an entrepôt. From there, they used traditional Chinese junks to carry produce for sale all around Puget Sound, as far away as Seattle. They also sold fruits and vegetables to merchant ships heading out to sea. Other Chinese gardeners formed another sixty-acre garden known as Station Prairie, near the old Fort Townsend.

Despite the success of these Chinese businesses, the cultural differences and language barriers continued to work against what was commonly called the Chinese Colony in Port Townsend. Some civic-minded folks made efforts to chip away at these divisions. A few churches in town offered English language classes for the Chinese. In 1886, Mark Ten Sui, a Christian from China who had been educated by the Methodist Church, opened his own English language school for local Chinese. Unfortunately, the school closed within a year. He moved back to Seattle and built a successful career there. After six years, he returned to Port Townsend and tried again, this time bringing along a Chinese minister from San Francisco. However, they could not generate much interest in Christianity among the Port Townsend Chinese.

Competing against the lure of Christianity were the traditional Chinese religions of Buddhism, Taoism, animism and other folk religions. The Chinese preferred to worship in their own temples, derisively dubbed by whites as "joss houses." (The term *joss* reportedly comes from *dios*, the Spanish word for God, or *deus*, the Portuguese word for God.)

The Chinese also tended to mete out justice against their own and handle other social issues their own way. One story describes an episode from 1892, when a Chinese man in Port Townsend came down with leprosy. Although leprosy was not particularly contagious, most people believed that it was. Local authorities tried to put him on a ship back to China, but the ship refused to take him on. The rumor quickly spread that the entire Chinese colony was infected with leprosy. Soon, some seamen reported that they had seen a boat full of Chinese occupants pass by in the night. They reported hearing a scream and a splash, and the man with leprosy was never seen again.

Not surprisingly, the white Christian community of Port Townsend had strenuous objections to the common use of opium among the Chinese. Opium was legal in the United States until 1914, but a brisk business in black market opium avoided the heavy import duties. Port Townsend's proximity to Victoria and its large opium processing factories made it a major conduit for opium smuggling into the United States.

Most Chinese opium smugglers were small-time—they tended to bring only enough opium from Victoria for personal use. The big-time smugglers tended to be whites, who were in it to make money. Many Chinese businesses had small opium dens at the rear of the store. Robert Gow, a longtime Chinese resident of Port Townsend, recalled watching men smoking in the back of the Ye Tung store. He described the opium den as having bunks and that there were always two or three men lying around smoking opium.

Around 1897, a fire consumed the heart of the Chinese colony, destroying one full block of buildings at today's Memorial Field at Madison and Water Streets. The fire department and numerous volunteers—both white and Chinese—fought to control the blaze but managed only to contain it to the one block. Investigators were never able to determine exactly how it

Port Townsend's Chinatown after it burned to the ground, on what is now the site of Memorial Field, at Washington and Madison Streets. The fire took place circa 1897. *Bert Kellogg Collection of the North Olympic Library System.*

Makeup and powder jars behind display glass. *From the collection at the Port Townsend Antique Mall; photo by the author.*

started, although many rumors circulated around town. Some said that two prostitutes were fighting and one flung a kerosene lamp at the other. Others said that young boys had started the fire.

Even before the fire that destroyed such a large chunk of the colony, the Chinese community in Port Townsend had dropped to about two hundred people by 1892. Some headed inland, away from the Pacific coast where prejudice against the Chinese was most intense. Others returned to China.

In 1911, the customs office moved to Seattle from Port Townsend, which eliminated Port Townsend as a port of entry for immigrating Chinese. By 1915, only a few Chinese were left in Port Townsend. The Zee Tai company continued to operate in town until 1930, when it was sold to a man named George Welch for $7,000. During that decade, the Chinese colony all but disappeared.

Postscript: In April 1990, almost one hundred years after Port Townsend's Chinese colony flourished at its peak, a pair of local merchants made a fascinating discovery. Bill and Kitty Sperry, who owned the Port Townsend

Antique Mall, were excavating the basement of their building. What they found both surprised and delighted them: artifacts from the daily life of Chinese residents who had lived there a century earlier. The Sperrys found bowls, coins, glass bottles and ceramic jugs, opium pipes, at least one opium tin, tools, hairbrushes, scraps of clothing, boar tusks and other household items. Today, a selection of the artifacts from the lost colony are on display at the Port Townsend Antiques Mall.

Chapter 10

THE PORT ANGELES RESURRECTION

Shangri-La, Spiritualism and Speculation

1880s

> *A well-matured Colonization Scheme. Permanent Employment in all branches of trade and industry at good wages, guaranteed. Free Lands, Water, Free Lights, Free Libraries, Exemption from taxes and Rents. All profits paid to Colonists. Town-site lands and fine harbor on Puget Sound, W.T.*[87]

Such was the extravagant promise from the "Projector and Gen'l Manager" George Venable Smith, signed with a flourish on the poster, just below a fetching pen-and-ink portrait of the neatly coiffed, mustachioed man himself.

Port Angeles had been snoozing along for the past twenty-five years since the great Valley Creek flood washed away the dreams of Victor Smith (not related to George). The population of white colonists had stayed mostly under fifty for much of that time. And then the colony came.

George Venable Smith had made it his mission to attract people to the Puget Sound Cooperative Colony by promising a Shangri-La, and he succeeded. The population of Port Angeles was "seventeen in 1883; four hundred in January 1890; one thousand in June 1890, when the place was incorporated as a town of the fourth-class."[88]

Six-year-old Madge Haynes arrived in the spring of 1887 with her parents, Mr. and Mrs. L.T. Haynes, when the colony was only fourteen days old. The family had sailed from the East Coast around Cape Horn at the tip of South America. They believed the rhapsodic brochures—at least little Madge had believed. She expected a "veritable paradise." Much later in life, Madge remembered instead, "[a]s we came up to the dock, we looked on shore and saw the pitifully few frame houses that faced on a street that was little better than a cowpath. It was certainly a dreary sight and most of the people took one look and wished they could go back where they came from."[89]

Alas, Madge said, most people had sold their homes to go live in the "Garden of Eden." There was no turning back, especially for those from faraway reaches in Scotland and England. The new arrivals covered some of the muddy "cowpath" with planks and put up a sawmill and several buildings near today's Ennis Creek. The new sawmill soon employed twenty people, and ships pulled up regularly to Morse Wharf and took away lumber.

Among the next wave of immigrants were Mr. and Mrs. James Burns, who had left the "soot and grime" of Birmingham, England. They were social progressives whose daughter Edna later spoke and wrote about her experiences growing up in the colony. Upon their arrival on a boat from Victoria, she said:

> *I saw men standing there dressed in a peculiar hunter's costume. Each put his head through a hole in the center of a blanket, then belted the blanket down around the waist.*
>
> *The men were without hats and wore their hair shoulder-length, carefully curled in ringlets…My parents lunched with Judge Smith that first day. He had the only safe in town and complained that so many persons brought him their money to keep he could not find room for his own.*[90]

Most of the colony had settled on the beach at Ennis Creek, about a mile east of what remained of the previous town, which was built around Valley Creek. As was the case during the Port Angeles of the 1860s, the Port Angeles of the 1880s was established near the site of an ancient Klallam village—this one was called I'e'nis. Most of the area was steep and heavily forested. A big chunk of that land still had the status of federal reservation, as it was designated by Abraham Lincoln during the 1860s. The colony headquarters was on the beach at the north end of Francis Street (today's Waterfront Park). A few feet inland was "a magnificent fir and cedar forest [that] came down to the shore everywhere one looked."[91]

By the time the Burns family arrived in February 14, 1888, the busy colonists had cleared timber and built four buildings, including one or more with a second floor of apartments. Colony leaders gave one of these apartments to the Burns family. James Burns worked as a carpenter, and his son worked at the sawmill. Within a few months, the family moved into their own house.

Colony board member Laura Hall quickly began publishing the colony newspaper, the *Model Commonwealth*, which she had brought with her from Seattle. Things weren't going too badly. Port Angeles was stirring back to life.

The events that woke up the sleeping settlement of Port Angeles started back in Seattle. Laborers were starting to organize, and they weren't happy with their wages or their working conditions. One of their loudest complaints focused on employers hiring cheap Chinese labor. A Seattle Knights of Labor organizer, Daniel Cronin, specifically pushed the "blame the Chinese" narrative.

The Puget Sound Cooperative was one of the primary groups inciting anti-Chinese resentment. Its agitation helped froth up the rage and hatred that brought on the riot of February 1886, when white laborers swarmed through the Chinese section of the city and forcibly abducted every Asian-looking person in sight. Historian John Putnam described the scene:

> *Sunday morning in Feb 1886, several hundred white working-class men and women gathered in the Chinese district in Seattle.*
>
> *On the pretense of enforcing local health regulations they pounded on doors, summarily condemned buildings, and strongly suggested that all Chinese leave the city. The Teamsters among the throng of white workers then hauled the outcasts' belongings to a nearby dock, where the Queen of the Pacific prepared to weigh anchor for its regular run to San Francisco. By the end of the morning approximately 350 Chinese residents—some frightened and others defiant—huddled together at the foot of the Queen's gangplank. The workers and spectators who milled around the docks then passed the hat to raise the $7 per head demanded by the ship's captain to transport the Chinese to California.*
>
> *The ship only had room for 200 passengers, and it filled up leaving 185 Chinese behind. One of the leaders of this mob was a man named George Venable Smith. At this point Smith insisted that the remaining Chinese be kept at the dock until another steamer arrived several days later. However, the local militia officers insisted that the remaining Chinese be escorted back to their residences in the Lava Beds district. While the escort was going on they encountered another group of workers at the corner of Maine and Commercial. They intervened and created a confrontation. One of the militia tried to arrest an unarmed logger and a scuffle ensued and five men were shot including the logger who was killed. The territorial governor declared martial law and federal troops arrived the next day.*[92]

About one year later, George Venable Smith, Laura Hall and several other Puget Sound Cooperative Colony leaders left Seattle to start their new colony on the Strait of Juan de Fuca. None had resolved the "Chinese question," but perhaps they felt they had left that issue behind in Seattle. They considered themselves progressive and were determined to build a utopian city where (white) people would live and work as a cooperative. There would be no employers.

The single female on the cooperative's board, Laura Hall, had been married previously to an alcoholic judge. She divorced the man in 1883 after he threatened to kill her during one of his frequent benders. She got involved with the cause when she met Peter Good. Good had recently visited France, where he toured the cooperative community at Guise. He wanted to model the Puget Sound Colony after the one in Guise. Laura Hall and Peter Good spent a great deal of time with George V. Smith, planning the Shangri-La that they would build on the Olympic Peninsula. Good died in 1886, a few months after the anti-Chinese riot. According to his friends, he had been imprisoned after the riot and never recovered physically.[93]

George Venable Smith, circa 1888. *Bert Kellogg Collection of the North Olympic Library System.*

Smith also faced consequences after the riot—almost. He was acquitted of conspiracy charges, and disbarment proceedings against him were unsuccessful. The *Seattle Times* newspaper denounced Smith and the others as "lackeys" of the hated Knights of Labor leader Daniel Cronin. The paper printed some choice and somewhat hysterical words directed at Smith: "George Venable Smith, you self styled brains of the lawless movement, you dupe of worse wire pullers… you are a socialist and an active socialist and a traitor to your country."[94]

"Wire-puller" and "socialist" or not, Smith himself was a diminutive figure with considerable ambition, aggressive racism and a strain of authoritarianism. He was a self-educated lawyer, born in 1843 in Kentucky. He had moved around a lot as a younger man, practicing law in California, Oregon, Utah and finally Washington, where he married May I. Vestal in 1880. It's not clear what he had done to generate such ire from the *Seattle Times*, but the newspaper also denounced the Puget Sound Cooperative idea, calling it a swindle that made "preposterous and impossible propositions to the dupes."

The colony leaders ignored their naysayers. They incorporated the cooperative and sold stock to those who wanted to buy in and move there. Stockholders became members of the cooperative and were expected to work. There were eleven trustees, with George V. Smith as president. The secretary was Albert E. Sanderson, a prominent socialist of the day.

In June 1886, colonists began to arrive at Port Angeles. In January 1887, twenty-two members were on site. Some of them had come from a high desert colony in Greeley, Colorado, perhaps looking for a place with more resources, including water.

The first few months brought only a trickle, but later that spring, larger parties began to arrive. From then on, the colony grew at a steady pace. A party of thirty-four arrived in April 1887 from Ohio and Chicago. Soon, large families arrived, including one with twelve children. These noisy families quickly became a flashpoint within the colony because each one brought many mouths to feed and only one or maybe two contributing workers (the father and perhaps sometimes the mother).

For the earliest arrivals, there was nowhere to stay. A hotel owned by David Morse filled quickly. Newcomers had to put up tents. By late that summer, the sawmill had cranked out 250,000 feet of lumber, but it still wasn't enough to build houses for all the colonists.

A fifty-dollar membership fee bought you a fifty-foot frontage lot. The first homes were built by colonists along today's East Front and First Streets, east of Peabody Street, up to the bluff. The colony headquarters was at the end of today's Francis Street. Colonists developed a communal garden at the north end of Ennis Creek Valley, today the abandoned Rayonier parking lot. The colony printed its own scrip, money that was accepted only at the colony store.

Laura Hall's work on the *Model Commonwealth* was mostly articles reprinted from various Knights of Labor papers. She peppered its pages with small encouragements, such as "We are, as colonists, equal with our brothers." She pushed for housewives in the colony to have the right to work outside the home for some portion of the day and earn their own money.

Perhaps shunned by her church after her divorce, Hall was a lapsed Christian. Like many "progressives" of the era and many other colony

Puget Sound Cooperative Colony scrip, circa 1888. It was good for use within the colony. *Bert Kellogg Collection of the North Olympic Library System.*

members, she considered herself a spiritualist, which was a popular pastime among sophisticated Victorians. At some later point, many from the colony gave up their fixation with spirituality and traded in their Saturday night séances for Sunday morning church. In direct contradiction to their original belief system, members of the colony eventually built several churches, including the First Congregational Church of Port Angeles.

A homeopathic physician arrived with a group of colonists and became the local doctor. He was assisted by a nurse and midwife known as Auntie Mackay. She was a tragic figure who had been left with five children after her husband died. Before she joined the colony, she also lost three of her children, and she then gave up the other two for adoption. She briefly married another colonist, but the marriage didn't work out. She became a well-known and treasured character in town, the "quaint little elderly lady with bright sparkling eyes and a friendly smile."[95]

The colony offered a busy social life—members had literary interests, along with music and theater. They created a library and started building an opera houses, plus a nursery and kindergarten. A rivalry developed between the older Port Angeles settlement, called the West End, and the colony, called the East End.

The winter of 1887–88 was a rough one, and some of the early arrivals left. Others abandoned the colony and its strictures, striking out on their own for private homesteads in the area. Meanwhile, as Port Angeles grew, so did the tensions and squabbles among the colonists and their leadership:

> *The board ran things, without much input from colonists, against their ideology. Within months, opposition to Smith's authoritarian leadership arose. In colony elections in September, Smith was returned to his position, but he had to rely on proxy votes from nonresident members for his majority. Most of the local voters—those closest to the situation—supported his opponent, E.B. Mastick. Laura* [Hall], *as part of the Smith faction, was also returned to office.*[96]

In August 1887, a teacher named Ione Tomlinson started a kindergarten for twenty-five children between the ages of three and eight. She also held afternoon classes for the older children. However, she had to fight hard to get the school opened with little support from the colony board. It lasted only two years and closed when a school opened in Port Angeles.

In April 1888, the colony trustees purchased twenty-five blocks of the Port Angeles townsite from Norman R Smith, who had inherited it from his father, Victor Smith. One of the trustees also procured an additional two hundred acres of timberland. The colony was growing but was also changing. The board election in 1888 went against both George Smith and Laura Hall. By then, both likely had their minds on other personal issues.

First colony buildings, at the mouth of Ennis Creek, Port Angeles, Washington, 1887. *Bert Kellogg Collection of the North Olympic Library System.*

Puget Sound Cooperative Colony buildings, 1887. The large building at the left is a hotel. *Bert Kellogg Collection of the North Olympic Library System.*

Puget Sound Cooperative Colony kindergarten, 1887. Teacher Ione Tomlinson Smith is in polka dots. *Bert Kellogg Collection of the North Olympic Library System.*

About one year after Laura Hall and her daughter arrived at the colony, a young Texan originally from Switzerland joined the group. Thirteen years younger than Hall, Charles J. Peters became interested in her, but he didn't care for the confines of colony rules. He soon left. He bought land in Port Angeles and set about homesteading. He and Laura married in 1888, and she joined him on the farm, which they dubbed Gyrenbad after his birthplace in Switzerland. After leaving the colony, she poured her energies into gardening and whipping up award-winning strawberry preserves. She held on to her populist roots, serving in 1896 as the Clallam County Populist delegate, the only woman at the statewide convention. She died in 1902 and was buried at Ocean View Cemetery in Port Angeles. A spiritualist minister conducted the service.

George Venable Smith, meanwhile, had become tangled up in a whirl of personal turmoil. His marriage to May Vestal ended when she left him for Norman Smith, an event that inspired rumors of wife-swapping among the colonists. In 1890, the now-divorced George Smith married Ione Tomlinson, the colony schoolteacher.

Born in 1847 in Connecticut, Ione's mother was Ann Northrop, whose American ancestry dated back to 1600s Connecticut, the time of the pilgrims. Her father was a prominent engineer, famous for building bridges and lighthouses. His ideals as an abolitionist and a Chartist (which called for universal voting rights) likely influenced his daughter Ione.

George Smith's second marriage to Ione Tomlinson was a solid one and lasted until his death in 1919, age seventy-six, in Port Angeles. He and Ione had one daughter, Lorna.

With at least two of the principal founders tossed out and otherwise engaged, the structure of the colony began to falter. In 1890, there were three thousand white settlers in the area, but not all were colony members. The town of Port Angeles was incorporated in June of that year. Although the 3,520-acre federal reserve was still off-limits, some squatters jumped the reserve. Finally, in 1891, new legislation opened up the land to homesteading.

Most colonists eventually built their own homes. The communal life that was supposed to sustain them did not last. The Haynes family—those early arrivals whose little girl, Madge, had expected a "veritable paradise"—managed the Dock Hotel for half a year and then homesteaded a farm west of town. They had a few precious cows and some chickens and lived in a log house. A few years later, they moved into town and built a house overlooking the strait at 114 North Peabody Street. Madge (Haynes) Nailor lived in the house her entire life.

Ione Tomlinson Smith, *on the right*, must have scandalized others given her habit of wearing pants while working outdoors. The man in the center is George Venable Smith. Photo circa 1887. *Bert Kellogg Collection of the North Olympic Library System.*

The business district of Port Angeles, circa 1890, facing Front and Oak Street, closer to the original townsite than the colony site. *Bert Kellogg Collection of the North Olympic Library System.*

The resiliency of the colony had been deeply compromised by squabbling among the leaders and their failure to live up to the absurd utopia that George V. Smith's posters had promised. It didn't take long for disappointed believers to leave in disgust or for others to give in to the temptations of the land grab.

When homesteading laws changed, that land grab went into full swing, with boisterous encouragement from former colonists. Much of the federal reserve had already been claimed by squatters. The capitalists and the speculators, in the end, took over. It was a land boom, with claims flying about and the homesteading stipulations still being ignored. Many bought land to subdivide and sell lots instead of farming. Everyone was going to be rich.

The colony dropped its pretense of being a social experiment and became a simple real estate business—or, in the eyes of its critics, a scheme of land speculators. Hoping for a great boom that never materialized, the colony ended up carrying huge debts, and it began the process of dying a slow death. Having failed as a Shangri-La, the colony then failed as a real estate corporation. The last full meeting of colonists apparently occurred at a Fourth of July picnic in 1889, an occasion that was visited by a freak summer snow.

Group of men and boys gathered for the official opening (for land claims) of the Port Angeles Townsite Reserve, 1892. *Bert Kellogg Collection of the North Olympic Library System.*

Port Angeles, however, did not die with the colony. There was no great land boom, but some made fortunes in the lumber business. Unfortunately, the silver panic of 1893 killed the only bank in town, but Port Angeles had developed enough economic stability to survive that blow. Gregers M. Lauridsen, a leading Port Angeles businessman, filled the gap by issuing his own money. "Lauridsen Money" remained a viable currency on the Olympic Peninsula for ten years.

George Venable Smith and Ione stayed in Port Angeles, where George enjoyed a long career working for the city. Over many years, he served as a probate judge, prosecuting attorney, city attorney and court commissioner.

Despite its short life and dubious claims to progressivism with its whites-only underpinnings, the Puget Sound Cooperative Colony was responsible for many "firsts" in Port Angeles, including the first sawmill, the first newspaper, the first schoolhouse (built in 1888, the site of the Washington School at First and Albert Streets), the first Protestant church, the first Congregational church, the first office building, the first (and only) opera house, the first steamer built in town (a sixty-ton steamer called the *Angeles*, launched on April 23, 1889), the first Catholic church, the first eight-hour workday and the first health and old age insurance.

In 1904, the colony sold the last of its land at auction and declared bankruptcy.

Chapter 11

THE MAGIC MAN OF MORA

1905–1935

Much like the frosty, unpredictable currents offshore from Rialto Beach, the stories about Claude Alexander Conlin usually take a wild, extravagant, even implausible turn. One might be forgiven for calling Conlin and the events of his dubious life "fishy."

Take the Gar Wood rumrunning speedboat story, recounted by a retired Canadian customs official named Martin Van Cooten. Conlin had quit his stage career and spent a great deal of time at his elaborate compound at Mora, overlooking the mouth of the Quillayute River and Rialto Beach. He was wealthy by then and perhaps bored, although his favorite hobby was fishing and there was plenty of it to be had. He was also dry because this event took place during the Prohibition years of the 1920s.

Famous and with plenty of celebrated contacts, Conlin had hired a noted speedboat racer and builder named Gar Wood to build him a custom boat. It had to be fast. Wood was no slouch and possibly rivaled Conlin in his showmanship. In a sensational stunt in 1925, he raced a train down the Hudson River from Albany to New York City, his boat, *Baby Gar IV*, beating the train by seventeen minutes. He had won five Gold Cup races and a Harmsworth Trophy, the "America's Cup" of speedboat racing.

Wood delivered Conlin's new boat to the latter's Mora compound, and Conlin put it to work immediately, running caches of illegal rum from Canada to Mora. But Conlin had at least one enemy who knew about

Split Rock at Rialto Beach. *Olympic National Park, National Park Service.*

the rumrunning. Perhaps he had a traitor among his hired help. Or it could have been a cuckolded husband from La Push whose wife had been meddled with by the notorious libertine. Either way, someone notified authorities, who set a trap.

Although the treacherous waters off Rialto Beach and throughout the Salish Sea required a highly skilled boat pilot, Alexander, at least on this occasion, drove the new speedboat himself. After picking up the rum, he was still in Canadian waters when he realized that he was being chased. His pursuers herded him into a narrow channel, where they had stretched a chain just below the surface of the water. The Canadian customs man, Van Cooten, claimed years later that Conlin's boat was going seventy miles

Gar Wood's speedboat, *Baby Gar IV*, after it beat the train from Albany to New York City. The boat he built for Conlin was built around the same time and was likely similar to *Baby Gar IV*. *Library of Congress, Prints and Photographs Division.*

per hour when it hit the submerged chain. It nearly sliced the beautiful new speedboat in half. Miraculously, the pilot was alive when they fished him out of the water. To their surprise, the authorities found that they had caught the man himself.

Rumrunning was a federal crime, and Conlin's Tacoma lawyers could not keep him out of the federal penitentiary on McNeil Island, despite the fact that he brought them a tin can stuffed with $30,000 in cash. However, Conlin was something of a magician, and he had spent a lifetime wriggling out of hopeless situations. He came up with a ridiculous plan to get himself out of McNeil as well.

Born in South Dakota in 1880, Claude Alexander Conlin moved with his family to Mount Vernon, Washington, when he was twelve. His father was a doctor, and Alexander had a brother, Clarence, and a sister, Benita. Alexander left home at a young age, making his first appearance as a teenager on stage at Dawson, Yukon, during the Klondike Gold Rush in 1898. He worked as a faro dealer in Dawson and performed on stage as someone who could walk through a wall made of ice blocks. He also developed a persona as a fortune teller who was good at telling eager gold rushers that they would soon be rich.

While in Alaska, Conlin befriended another soon-to-be famous showman of the era, Alexander Pantages, who later ran a string of vaudeville theaters in Seattle. Conlin's biographer makes an unsubstantiated case that Pantages and Conlin were both involved in the shooting death of the Wild West's most infamous and ubiquitous huckster, Soapy Smith. At that time, Soapy Smith was making the rounds of Klondike gold rush towns, conning and extorting gold miners. Smith had supposedly threatened to kill Pantages, and late in life, Pantages was quoted as saying that he owed Alexander Conlin his life. However, it's not clear what Pantages was referring to. Most historians agree that it was another man who shot Smith and that there is no evidence that either Conlin or Pantages were involved in any way.

What is verifiable is that, around 1902, Conlin left Alaska and returned to Seattle, where he soon established himself as "Alexander the Great," a medium and psychic. Alexander possessed the added bonus of being a charismatic showman who was particularly engaging to women. During these early days as a performer, he partnered with several other vaudeville acts, including a cowboy magician who could make a birdcage disappear and a hypnotist named Jester.

In the spring of 1902, at age twenty-two, Conlin met and married a young lady from St. Louis named Jessie M. Culler (or Cullen). The first of many marriages for Conlin, this one lasted less than a year. However, he quickly recovered from that breakup when he met a fourteen-year-old girl in Los Angeles. He and young Ethel Lyman eloped, and Ethel became part of his stage act when he taught her how to escape from handcuffs. In 1906, they welcomed a son, Claude Alexander Conlin Jr. Dragging wife and son along with him, Conlin began touring around the American Southwest, taking on the nickname of the "Handcuff King." He soon added mind reading as part of his show. He gained enough repute to catch the attention of, and get a very bad review from, the famed Harry Houdini.

At some point, Ethel grew tired of the nomad life and returned to L.A. with young Alexander Jr. She later said that her husband had been physically abusive and manipulative. But Conlin had already moved on with a seventeen-year-old San Francisco girl named Della Martell, whom he married in the summer of 1907. He did fail to mention to Della that he was still married to Ethel. He gathered up his new wife and headed east, where wife number three was less likely to learn about the existence of wife number two. (It's unclear whether or not he had actually divorced wife number one.)

At this point in his career, he realized that he needed to find something to make himself stand out better among the throngs of hucksters, con

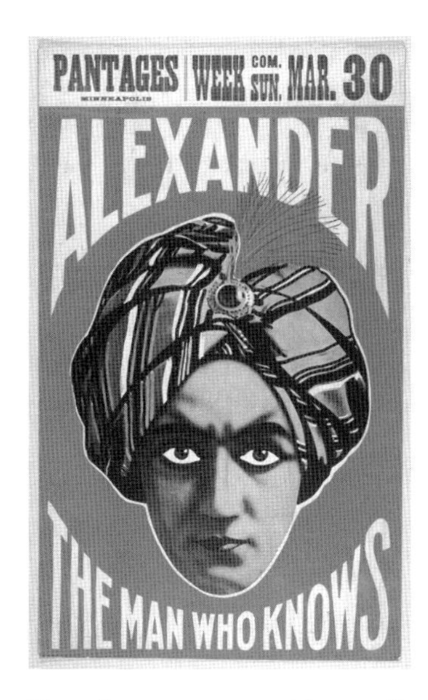

One of many posters, with one of many names, that Conlin created to advertise and promote himself. *Library of Congress, Prints and Photographs Division.*

artists and magicians who crowded the vaudeville circuit. He had cards printed up calling himself Alexander the Magician, "a high-class entertainer." This persona soon evolved into "Astro, the White Mahatma." Eventually, a stage name that stuck was "Astro: The Man Who Knows."

As part of his act, Conlin asked his audience to write questions that were then put into envelopes and ostensibly left on a table on stage. His costume included an oversized feathered turban, which hid a newfangled wireless setup. This allowed his assistant—backstage with the actual questions—to read them into a microphone while Conlin pretended to "divine" the contents of the empty envelopes sitting on the table in front of him. The other part of the show was Conlin hypnotizing his wife, who then answered the questions. A critic later wrote that the "answers" were vague enough and delivered with enough confidence that people accepted them. If anyone challenged the answer, Conlin would bully them into submission. This routine was convincing enough that Alexander and Della developed a side business doing private readings.

In November 1909, Alexander and Della got a little greedy and tried a more elaborate and focused con. A wealthy tugboat tycoon from Oregon named O'Kelly lost his wife and wanted to find his stepdaughter, the deceased wife's daughter from her previous marriage. He had made a deathbed promise to his dying wife that he would make sure the girl got the money her mother was leaving her. The girl had left home before her mother married O'Kelly, and the widower had never met her. Conlin heard about the tycoon and did some research before meeting with him. He approached O'Kelly and offered to help with a séance. He had O'Kelly remove his coat and vest and then went into a trance. To O'Kelly's amazement, Conlin correctly told him that the girl's name was Lillie Wittman, and then he gave the grieving widower an address and said she was going by the assumed name of Stella Mason.

The next morning, O'Kelly arrived at the address and was greeted by a young woman who jumped into his arms crying "Oh, Father!" O'Kelly wondered how the young miss could recognize him, since the two had never met. When he asked for proof of her identity, she produced a picture of his dead wife, which removed his doubts.

She confided that she had always dreamed of attending music school in New York, so he gave her $546 in gold and bought her a train ticket. She promised to repay him when her mother's estate was settled. He then took her shopping for clothes and jewelry and gave her the precious belongings of her dead mother. He handed her a pile of stamped postcards so she could be sure to write to him along her way to the New York music school and sent her off at the train station.

He waited five days without word before taking his growing suspicions to the police. They went back to Conlin's "Astro the White Mahatma" parlor on Market Street, where they found Alexander and Della, also known as Stella Mason, along with a toddler.

Della broke down and confessed that she had swiped the photograph of the man's dead wife from his vest pocket and made a copy. Alexander and Della, along with a third accomplice, were charged with grand larceny, and their pictures appeared in newspapers up and down the West Coast. Conlin's wife number two, Ethel Conlin, saw the story, including mention of the child. She hopped on the next train from Los Angeles to San Francisco, where she went immediately to the police and informed them that, six weeks prior, her husband had kidnapped her three-year-old son, Alexander Jr., during an arranged visit.

During the ensuing kerfuffle, Della Conlin realized that she was not actually married to Alexander and that his previous wife, Ethel, had not, in fact, died in childbirth, as Alexander had told her when he came home with little Alexander.

The outraged young Della soon testified against her fake husband, saying that he had beaten her numerous times and that she had tried but failed to leave him:

> *If I have done wrong and they wish to punish me, I suppose that I must be punished. That's all I did, what Astro told me to do and I could not resist him. It seems pretty hard for a young girl, who really wants to do the right thing. I'm married to Astro because he was nice to me at first. I wanted to lead a good life. I have never wanted anything else. I was deceived and I cannot help it now. If the authorities see fit to be lenient with me, I will go to Los Angeles for my mother and will put Astro out of my mind.*[97]

Mr. O'Kelly says he doesn't want to prosecute me. He knows that I had to do what Astro ordered. He says he will spend every cent that he owns to punish Astro. However, Mr. O'Kelly knew that I took the money from him and that I wanted to spend it to go to Los Angeles. He isn't angry about that. He knows of my plight.[98]

From there, the story took several improbable turns: Alexander and Della returned home together without the child. The next day, Alexander and his brother, Clarence, took Della to the hospital, after which she was transferred to the Adler sanatorium. A doctor diagnosed Della as suffering from "internal diseases" requiring surgery, which would unfortunately prevent her from further testifying.

Meanwhile, poor Mr. O'Kelly began to experience strange visitations at his San Francisco apartment, including "cabalistic signs and messages appearing on the doors and walls of his rooms."[99] Police concluded that these ghostly visits were actually made by friends of Conlin, and they assigned police protection to O'Kelly.

Soon, two other cases popped up against Conlin. One young lady had been promised a 6 percent return if she invested her entire savings of $250 in a mine. An actor was swindled out of $200.

Meanwhile, Conlin bolted. He quickly reappeared in different newspaper headlines, this time in the South. He was captured in Arkansas but made another escape, allegedly with the help of Della and his brother Clarence, a California attorney. He was caught yet again, and newspapers reported that he had been shot during the arrest. He was close to death, so authorities dropped all charges. Remarkably, he did not die but instead lived on to get into even more trouble. Within a few months, he was arrested in Mississippi for stealing jewelry from an "intimate" friend who claimed to be his wife. At the same time, he went on trial for conning $10,000 from a young man whose wife had hired "Astro, the Healer of Hearts" to heal hers. Instead, she got arrested as an accomplice to the con against her husband and was served with a divorce.

Conlin did a good number of interviews during these ongoing shenanigans and always came off as lighthearted and amused by all the fake charges brought by great liars who kept trying to nab him. He obviously enjoyed the attention.

Conlin's biographer reported that around this time, Conlin killed a Black man after an alleged attack outside a stage door somewhere. If the story is true, the newspapers that had been reporting on his ongoing misdeeds did not report the killing.

In May 1912, Conlin was arrested in New Orleans for "conducting a notorious clairvoyant parlor."[100] In September of that year, he interrupted his relationship with Della to marry a Zora Lennour (or Lenore), but they reportedly divorced a short time later and he remarried Della in 1914. That final marriage was short-lived.

In February 1914, the old O'Kelly charges resurfaced after California authorities realized that he wasn't dead after all or wasn't in prison for all the various other charges he had faced. He paid a fine and resumed his career, which had him now as an authentic eastern mystic who could read people's minds and tell the future. He had further developed his skill at giving advice to women on matters of the heart. He advertised himself widely in newspapers and posters.

At some point, he discovered a pair of nineteen-year-old twins named Marguerite and Marie Johnson who had been trained as dancers. Their mother was a struggling widow and was happy to let them dress up on stage in exotic far eastern outfits and perform the "Crystal Dance of India," along with other seductive pieces. They quickly became known as the Nartell Twins as a regular part of his show. They also became the subject of one of Alexander's new hobbies: photography. They appear nude in at least one photograph taken by Conlin, although they are posed in such a way that little is revealed.

In addition to the wireless receiver concealed in his turban, Conlin also began using a hidden microphone installed in the powder room of various theaters. The banter was monitored by an assistant, who would jot down any conversations that could be used in Conlin's mind reading performances.

At the end of 1915, he married once again, this time to Lillian Bartlett. Lillian quickly became part of his stage show, one of the trio of alluring young ladies who adorned his magical and cabalistic performances.

Around this time, a brief story about Conlin appeared in the *Oregon Daily Journal* on October 27, 1916. The story describes the magician, "Alexander the Great," kidnapping a ten-year-old boy, Wilford, from the home of probation officer Charles Parks:

> *Alexander claims the child is his and was taken from him in San Francisco two years ago when he was overpowered by three thugs.*
>
> *The child was taken to the jail yesterday and thence to the juvenile jail, where Parkes stole him away again and rode off on a motorcycle.*
>
> *Parkes says the child's mother, Alexander's former wife, was Parkes' niece. She died three years ago, he says, and left the child to him. Alexander claimed he had been searching for the child for two years.*[101]

Based on the dates, the mother could have been an unknown paramour, since the birth date of young Wilford Parks would have been the same year as Ethel's and Alexander's son, Claude Alexander Conlin Jr. The newspapers did not follow up on the story, so it is unknown whether the boy ended up staying with his uncle or who his mother was.

Over the following years, Conlin began making serious money. Traveling with his show around the Pacific Northwest with his trio of lovelies in 1919, he made $18,000, which in today's money is about $314,000. In one week in Vancouver, British Columbia, the gross take was $9,000—an enormous amount of money for two weeks of work. One of his most profitable gigs was private consultations with women, some of whom swooned over him and offered to father his children. He wasn't above having secret "readings" with some of these women when Lillian wasn't around.

Whenever he needed time off, Conlin headed out to Mora to enjoy his favorite pastimes of hunting and fishing. In the early years at Mora, beginning around 1905, he spent his summer months there, camping at first. It was remote and difficult to access at the time, either by boat or via a primitive road.

At Mora, K.O. Erickson, a well-known pioneer, had built a trading post in the 1880s and later opened a post office. Erickson eventually leased his holdings to J.E.L. James, a former saloon keeper in Seattle and sea captain. James built the Hotel Mora overlooking the Quillayute and told others about his great hopes for the area. He bragged that there was also a dance hall near his hotel, but its remote location kept it from thriving. James had also been part of the Klondike Gold Rush, and he and Conlin quickly became good friends, hunting and fishing together. Some of James's hotel guests were reportedly disreputable—perhaps hiding from authorities. But "Alexander was in his element and enjoyed playing the role of raconteur around the hotel dinner table"[102]

Conlin insisted that the three constant females in his life (Lillian and the Nartell Twins) go hunting and fishing with him, although they preferred to stay at the hotel. Sometimes these trips required them to put together the tents in the camps and serve up the fruits of the hunting and fishing expeditions.

In 1918, as more cash rolled in, he began planning his own Mora compound. He chose a quiet inlet overlooking the beach where the Quillayute River poured into the ocean. At low tide, one could walk across the rocky base of the inlet, but it was cut off at high tide. His building site on the steep hillside facing the ocean became known as "Alexander's island."

Boston on Quillayute, later renamed Mora, 1880s. *Bert Kellogg Collection of the North Olympic Library System.*

Hotel Mora and the post office at Mora, Washington, early twentieth century. *Bert Kellogg Collection of the North Olympic Library System.*

He announced that the beach would be known as Rialto Beach, a reference to his life in the common man's theater.

The construction project for his compound was a difficult one. Transporting materials and manpower to the site was at times impossible. Rain and gale-force winds in the winter months hammered the bluff. But slowly the estate began to take shape. The large main house, with an enclosed porch facing the ocean, "rivaled anything constructed in Port Townsend or Seattle. It was resplendent with expensive tapestries and antiques. Exotic plants were brought in from all over the world."[103]

He built gardens, an elaborate footpath and rock terraces, two guest houses, a caretaker's cottage and several special-purpose tree houses.

It was said that Conlin did not believe in banks and that he kept his earnings in cash, stuffed into tin cans and buried around his various properties. And there was a lot of money. By 1919, his show was bringing in as much as a Broadway show in ticket prices and attendance. He was heavily booked to the point that he collapsed from exhaustion. He took time off to travel to Europe and rest up at Mora. He also began developing less rigorous income streams, including books that gave up his magic secrets and a customized Ouija board. He invented a mysterious "author" who published a book called *The Life and Mysteries of the Celebrated Dr. "Q"* and offered it exclusively to gullible customers on a mailing list. He also started a mail-order business where customers sent him three questions, which he would answer for a fee. He published another nine-hundred-page book called *The Inner Secrets of Psychology*, consisting of "practical advice and mumbo jumbo blended into an early self-help format."[104]

Yet another book arrived under the pen name Swami Bhakta Ishita called *The Development of Seership*. Throughout the early 1920s, he cranked out his books and spent more time at Mora and traveling to Europe—and rumrunning.

Sometimes, at Mora, he invited widows to his home for private séances in his tree houses. The widows paid to spend the night in the tree houses, where their departed husbands would speak to them. Unbeknownst to the widows, the talking tree houses were wired with hidden microphones and speakers.

Rumors began to spread among the hardscrabble locals about the strange goings-on at the compound, especially the steady traffic of women. One story circulated that someone had set up a predator trap and that Conlin's Siamese cat got stuck in it and was killed. The man was afraid of Conlin, so he tried to hide the evidence. Locals spread gossip about brothels and orgies and the smuggling of Chinese immigrants, not to mention the rumrunning. One local reportedly had a gun battle with Conlin over the

Unidentified woman standing in front of Alexander Conlin's house at Rialto Beach. *Fannie Taylor Collection at Olympic National Park, National Park Service.*

latter's relationship with the man's stepmother. No one was hurt, and it's not clear how much of the gossip was invented.

In 1926, Conlin was again in trouble with the law when he tried to blackmail a rich oil man with evidence of the man's illicit affair. Allegedly, Conlin threatened to kill the man and his twenty-one-year-old daughter. The man went to the police, and Conlin was arrested. In the end, Conlin again walked away a free man. His biographer speculated that he had bribed the attorney general.

After a final season on the Pantages theater circuit in 1927, Conlin decided to retire from the stage. He was forty-seven years old and had millions of dollars, much of it stashed in tin cans around the Mora property and his other homes. His grandson told interviewers that he recalled a secret panel inside of a vanity cabinet containing $330,000 in cash. He did use banks to some extent, according to his son, who claimed that he once had to carry $200,000 in cash home from a visit to a bank.

Conlin soon reinvented himself into a "financier," operating a "personal loan" service, charging interest as high as 40 percent. His son remembered, "Dad was a nice guy, unless somebody missed one of their payments."[105]

Conlin did not escape the eventual notice of the Internal Revenue Service, which arrested him in 1928 for tax evasion. In the end, he paid a large settlement of $77,500.

In 1929, Lillian filed for divorce after fourteen years. She had two kids, John and Gloriana, and she was tired of his "nefarious ways." He failed to show up to the divorce hearing, and she was granted the divorce by default.

It was during the '20s that Conlin also began his bootlegging career. The location of his home on Rialto Beach was perfect for running booze from Canada just forty miles away.

After he was arrested in the Gar Wood speedboat, Conlin lost his case and was sentenced to a term at McNeil Island Federal Penitentiary. While incarcerated, Conlin complained of stomach pain, and he was diagnosed as having terminal pancreatic cancer. Shortly after that, he was released to live out his final days at home.

It wasn't long before a miraculously cured Conlin bought a lovely home in Seattle. He never lived in the house, but he did employ his former McNeil prison guard as a caretaker. It's not clear whether he also thanked the prison doctor for the diagnosis as generously as he thanked the guard with the free house.

In 1930, Conlin married again, to a woman named Grace Coughlin. This marriage ended four years later in 1934, the same year that Conlin's Mora compound mysteriously burned to the ground. The rumor spread at La Push that the fire had been set by the husband of one of Conlin's paramours—or perhaps attempted paramours. He never rebuilt the home. Today, the property shows very little sign of the "castle" that once existed there—only a set of stairs and the remains of the foundation hidden away in the heavy brush.

Conlin spent the rest of his life in one or the other of fourteen homes he owned. He may or may not have married Myrdith Mortensen in 1943 in Chihuahua, Mexico. He reportedly had a companion named Carmen Jaquinta, who was twenty-seven years old to his seventy years. He died in Seattle in 1954. As per Conlin's wishes, his son scattered his ashes at Rialto Beach.

NOTES

Chapter 1

1. Bishop, oral history.
2. MacDonald, *The Egg and I*, 50.
3. Ibid.
4. Becker, *Looking for Betty MacDonald*, 40.
5. Ibid., 46.
6. Ibid., 48.
7. Ibid., 124.
8. Ibid., 113.
9. Ibid., 119.

Chapter 2

10. Quileute Nation, "Quileute History."
11. Center for the Study of the Pacific Northwest, "History of Treaty Making and Reservations."
12. Ibid.
13. Brackbill, *Queen of Heartbreak Trail*, 126.
14. Ibid., 127.
15. Ibid., 128.
16. Ibid.

17. Ibid., 129.
18. Ibid.
19. Ibid.
20. Quileute Nation, "Quileute History."
21. Center for the Study of the Pacific Northwest, "Treaty Making and Reservations on the Olympic Peninsula: A Suspicious Fire."
22. Brackbill, *Queen of Heartbreak Trail*, 149.
23. Ibid., 159.
24. Ibid.
25. Ibid., 215.
26. Ibid., 218.

Chapter 3

27. "Horrible Affair at New Dungeness," 1.
28. Ibid.
29. Washington State Archives, Jefferson Frontier Justice, case number 468; JEF-457.
30. Duncan, "Dungeness Massacre."
31. Ibid.
32. "In Memoriam," 1.
33. Ibid.

Chapter 4

34. Gruen, "Ozette Archaeological Site."
35. Steury, "Home of My Family."
36. Ibid.
37. Ibid.
38. Daugherty, Ozette Archaeological Expedition.
39. "Civilization Lost…and Found."
40. Gruen, "Ozette Archaeological Site."
41. Steury, "Home of My Family."
42. "Civilizations Lost…and Found."
43. "Civilizations Lost…and Found."
44. Daugherty, Ozette Archaeological Expedition.

Chapter 5

45. "Dreadful Calamity," 1.
46. Campbell, *History of the North Olympic Peninsula*.
47. Ramsey, "How the Civil War Played Out."
48. Kendall, "Strange Customs of Victor Smith."
49. Ibid.
50. Morgan, *Last Wilderness*, 47, 48.
51. Ibid.
52. Ibid.
53. Ibid.
54. Ibid.
55. Ibid.
56. *Washington Standard*, June 2, 1864, 2.
57. Kendall, "Strange Customs of Victor Smith."
58. Smith, "Victory," 136.
59. Ibid., 131.
60. Leighton, *West Coast Journeys*, 22.

Chapter 6

61. (Beecher), "Biggest Opium Seizure on Record," 2.
62. Harriet Beecher Stowe Center, "Stowe's Global Impact."
63. "Following Special from Washington," 1.
64. "Beechers in Trouble," page 2, column 2.
65. "Where Is Beecher?," 1.
66. "Beecher's Statement," 1.
67. *Evening Telegraph*, January 7, 1887, 4.
68. *Spokane Falls Review*, July 14, 18887, 3.
69. *Puget Sound Argus*, July 14, 1887, 3.
70. *Seattle Post-Intelligencer*, June 22, 1888, 5.
71. "To Be Rid of Beecher," 4.
72. *Puget Sound Argus*, April 18, 1889, 1.
73. (Beecher), "Thieves of the Custom Service," 1.
74. (Beecher), "Loss of the Libby," 1.
75. *Seattle Post-Intelligencer*, December 30, 1889, 1.

Chapter 7

76. Swan, "Diary of James Swan," January 12, 1864.
77. Ibid.
78. Reagan and Walters, "Tales from the Hoh and Quileute," 297–346.
79. Ibid., 322.
80. Atwater et al., "Orphan Tsunami of 1700."
81. Ibid.
82. Spitz, "How Scientists Know."
83. Garrison-Laney and Miller, "Tsunamis in the Salish Sea."
84. Atwater et al., "Orphan Tsunami of 1700," 93.

Chapter 8

85. Clark, "Smoke Makes Nightmarish Scene," 1.
86. Amundson, "On 60th Anniversary Today."

Chapter 10

87. Smith, "Well-Matured Colonization Scheme," poster.
88. Bradley, *O'Toole's Mallet*.
89. "Co-Op Way of Life."
90. Ibid.
91. Ibid.
92. Putnam, "Racism and Temperance," 70–81.
93. Cloud, "Laura Hall Peters," 28–36.
94. LeWarne, *Utopias on Puget Sound*, 18.
95. Ibid., 39.
96. Cloud, "Laura Hall Peters."

Chapter 11

97. Charvet and Pomeroy, *Alexander*, 53.
98. Ibid., 54.
99. Ibid.
100. Ibid., 59.

101. "'Alexander' Figures in a Kidnapping," 2.
102. Charvet and Pomeroy, *Alexander*, 169.
103. Ibid.
104. Ibid., 163.
105. Ibid., 180.

BIBLIOGRAPHY

Books

Becker, Paula. *Looking for Betty MacDonald: The Egg, the Plague, Mrs. Piggle-Wiggle, and I*. Seattle: University of Washington Press, 2016.

Brackbill, Eleanor Phillips. *The Queen of Heartbreak Trail: The Life and Times of Harriet Smith Pullen, Pioneering Woman*. Essex, CT: Two Dot Box, 2021.

Bradley, Thomas H. *O'Toole's Mallet on the Resurrection of the Second National City of the United States of America*. Port Angeles, WA: Calvert Company, 1894.

Campbell, Patricia. *A History of the North Olympic Peninsula*. N.p.: Peninsula Publishing, 1979.

Charvet, David, and John Pomeroy. *Alexander: The Man Who Knows*. Pasadena, CA: Mike Caveney's Magic Words, 2004.

Leighton, Caroline. *West Coast Journeys, 1865–1879*. Reprint, Seattle, WA: Sasquatch Books, 1995.

LeWarne, Charles. *Utopias on Puget Sound*. Seattle: University of Washington Press, 1975.

MacDonald, Betty. *The Egg and I*. New York: J. Lippincott Inc., 1945.

Morgan, Murray. *The Last Wilderness*. Seattle: University of Washington Press, 2019.

Russell, Jervis. *Jimmy Come Lately: History of Clallam County: A Symposium*. Port Angeles, WA: Clallam County Historical Society, 1971.

Newspaper and Magazine Articles

"'Alexander' Figures in a Kidnapping." *Oregon Daily Journal*, October 27, 1916.

Amundson, Mavis. "On 60th Anniversary Today, Great Forks Fire Still Sparks Legend for Valiant Efforts." *Peninsula Daily News*, September 20, 2011.

Atwater, Brian F., Musumi-Rokkaku Satoko, Satake Kenji, Tsuji Yoshinobu, Ueda Kazue and David K. Yamaguchi. "The Orphan Tsunami of 1700. Japanese Clues to a Parent Earthquake in North America, Second Edition." *United States Geological Survey, in Association with University of Washington Press. Prepared in Cooperation with the Geological Survey of Japan (National Institute of Advanced Industrial Science and Technology), the University of Tokyo, and the University of Washington*. 2015.

(Beecher). "Biggest Opium Seizure on Record." *Daily British Colonist*, January 20, 1886.

———. "Loss of the Libby." *Puget Sound Argus*, November 14, 1889.

———. *Puget Sound Argus* 18, no. 21 (July 1, 1886).

———. *Seattle Post-Intelligencer*, December 30, 1889.

———. *Seattle Post-Intelligencer*, June 22, 1888.

———. *Spokane Falls Review*, July 14, 1887.

———. "Thieves of the Custom Service." *Yakima Herald*, April 18, 1889.

———. *Yakima Herald*, April, 1889.

"The Beechers in Trouble." *Puget Sound Argus*, April 29, 1886.

"Beecher's Statement." *Evening Telegraph*, September 15, 1886.

(Blake). "In Memoriam." *Port Townsend Argus*, May 11, 1871.

Clark, Earl. "Smoke Makes Nightmarish Scene in Battle to Save Forks." *Olympic Tribune*, September 21, 1951.

Cloud, Barbara, and Laura Hall Peters. "Pursuing the Myth of Equality." *Pacific Northwest Quarterly* 74, no. 1 (January 1983). https://www.jstor.org/stable/40490746.

"The Co-Op Way of Life—as Remembered by Madge Nailor." *The Shield* (Spring 1969).

Daugherty, Richard. The Ozette Archaeological Expedition, a cooperative project of Makah Nation, Washington State University, National Park Service, National Science Foundation, Bureau of Indian Affairs. http://npshistory.com/publications/olym/oae-overview.pdf.

"A Dreadful Calamity. Destruction of the Town of Port Angeles by a Landslide—Loss of Life." *Oregon Statesman*, January 4, 1864.

Evening Telegraph. January 7, 1887.

"The Following Special from Washington to the Detroit Free Press Is Decidedly Interesting." *Puget Sound Argus*, July 22, 1886.

Garrison-Laney, Carrie, and Ian Miller. "Tsunamis in the Salish Sea: Recurrence, Sources, Hazards." *Geological Society of America Field Guide* 49 (July 20, 2017).

"A Horrible Affair at New Dungeness." *Washington Standard*, July 16, 1864.

Liestman, Daniel. "'The Various Celestials Among Our Town': Euro-American Response to Port Townsend's Chinese Colony." *Pacific Northwest Quarterly* 85, no. 3 (July 1994). https://www.jstor.org/stable/40491474.

"Mosaics of the City." Unidentified newspaper at North Olympic Library System Archives, January 1893.

(Ozette). "Civilization Lost…and Found." *Washington Post*, June 24, 1979.

Puget Sound Argus. April 18, 1889.

———. July 14, 1887.

Putnam, John. "Racism and Temperance: The Politics of Class and Gender in Late 19th-Century Seattle." *Pacific Northwest Quarterly* 95, no. 2 (Spring 2004): 70–81. https://www.jstor.org/stable/40491731.

Ramsey, Bruce. "How the Civil War Played Out in Washington Territory." *Seattle Times*, July 2, 2013.

Reagan, Albert B., and L.V.W. Walters. "Tales from the Hoh and Quileute." *Journal of American Folklore* 46, no. 182 (October–December 1933). https://www.jstor.org/stable/535636.

Seattle Post-Intelligencer. June 22, 1888.

Spokane Falls Review. July 14, 1887.

Steury, Tim. "The Home of My Family: Ozette, the Makahs, and Doc Daugherty." *Washington State Magazine* (Spring 2008).

"To Be Rid of Beecher." *Seattle Post-Intelligencer*, November 28, 1888.

Washington Standard. June 2, 1864.

"Where Is Beecher?" *Tacoma Evening Telegraph*, September 10, 1886.

Online Articles

Center for the Study of the Pacific Northwest. "A History of Treaty Making and Reservations on the Olympic Peninsula." https://www.washington.edu/uwired/outreach/cspn/Website/Classroom%20Materials/Curriculum%20Packets/Treaties%20&%20Reservations/III.html.

———. "Treaty Making and Reservations on the Olympic Peninsula: A Suspicious Fire," https://www.washington.edu/uwired/outreach/cspn/

Website/Classroom%20Materials/Curriculum%20Packets/Treaties%20&%20Reservations/III.html.

Dougherty, Phil. "Mobs Forcibly Expel Most of Seattle's Chinese Residents Beginning on February 7, 1886." HistoryLink, November 17, 2013. https://www.historylink.org/file/2745.

Duncan, Kathy. "Dungeness Massacre." Jamestown S'Klallam Tribe, "The Strong People." jamestowntribe.org/history/hist_massacre.htm.

Gruen, J. Philip. "Ozette Archaeological Site." SAH Archipedia. https://sah-archipedia.org/buildings/WA-01-009-0042.

Harriet Beecher Stowe Center. "Stowe's Global Impact: Her Words Changed the World." https://www.harrietBeecherstowecenter.org/harriet-Beecher-stowe/her-global-impact.

Kendall, John. "The Strange Customs of Victor Smith." Clallam Historical Society. https://www.clallamhistoricalsociety.com/data/Collections/Articles/The%20Strange%20Customs%20of%20Victor%20Smith%20Chapter%201.pdf.

Olympic Peninsula Community Museum. "The Great Forks Fire of 1951." https://content.lib.washington.edu/cmpweb/exhibits/forksfire/index.html.

Quileute Nation. "Quileute History." https://quileutenation.org/history.

Spitz, Tullan. "How Scientists Know When the Last Cascadia Earthquake Happened." Oregon Public Broadcasting, Portland, Oregon, January 26, 2015. https://www.opb.org/news/series/unprepared/jan-26-1700-how-scientists-know-when-the-last-big-earthquake-happened-here.

Interview

Edward "Bud" LeRoy Bishop. Oral history, 1992. Jefferson County Historical Society.

Archives

Washington State Archives, Jefferson Frontier Justice. Case Number: 468; JEF-457.

Manuscripts

Coventon, Kathleen. "History of the Puget Sound Cooperative Colony." Unpublished 1939 manuscript, University of Washington Library, Seattle.
Smith, Norman. "Victory." Unpublished manuscript, North Olympic Library System Archives, Port Angeles, Washington.
Swan, James. "Diary of James Swan." January 12, 1864. Pacific Norwest Seismic Network, https://pnsn.org/outreach/native-american-stories/other-stories/james-swan-s-diary. Diary available at University of Washington Manuscripts Collection, accession no. 1703-001.

Poster

Smith, George Venable. "A Well-Matured Colonization Scheme." Promotional poster. North Olympic Library System archives room in Port Angeles, Washington.

ABOUT THE AUTHOR

Carol Turner is the author of *Scoundrels of the Salish Sea*, *Forgotten Heroes and Villains of Sand Creek*, *The Trouble with Heather Holloway* and other books. She was educated at Sonoma State University and Bennington College. She lives in Port Angeles, Washington, with two spoiled greyhounds.